Stained Glass Mosaics
Original Projects for Beginners

Sigalit Eshet

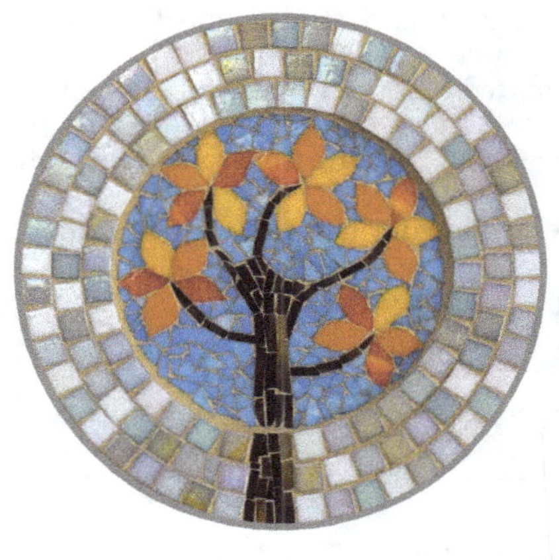

Photographs by Efrat Tenenbaum and Sigalit Eshet

Translation: AQ Group | https://www.aqenglish.com/

ISBN: 978-965-92633-8-7

www.sigalitart.net/en

Disclaimer

All do-it-yourself activities involve risk, and your safety is your own responsibility, including proper use of equipment and safety gear, and determining whether you have adequate skill and experience.

Some of the resources used for these projects are dangerous unless used properly and with adequate pre-cautions, including safety gear.

Some illustrative photos do not depict safety precautions or equipment, in order to show the project step more clearly.

Some projects are user-submitted, and appearance of a project in this format does not indicate it has been checked for safety or functionality. Use of the instructions and suggestions is at your own risk.

I disclaim all responsibility for any resulting damage, injury, or expense. It is your responsibility to make sure that your activities comply with all applicable laws.

Content:

Introduction ... 4

Why Glass? ... 6

Glass Mosaic tools and equipment ... 7

Preparation tools ... 8

Grout ... 9

Safety instructions ... 9

The Glass ... 10

Adhesives ... 12

Project No. 1: Colorful Tile Tray ... 13

Project No. 2: Spiral ... 17

Cutting glass tiles ... 19

Project No. 3: Candle Holder ... 21

Cutting Glass with a Nipper ... 24

Project No. 4: Butterfly ... 25

Gluing Glass ... 29

Project No. 5: Blue Picture Frame ... 30

Cutting Glass with Glass Cutter ... 33

Project No. 6: Square Mirror ... 34

Cutting Glass into Thin Strips ... 37

Project No. 7: Round Picture ... 38

Cutting Glass into Shapes and Using the Pliers ... 42

Project No. 8: Colorful Fishy Tray ... 44

Project No. 9: Colorful Picture ... 48

Project No. 10: Mandala ... 51

Project No. 11: Color Gradient ... 56

Project No. 12: Leftover Glass Garden Pot ... 60

Project No. 13: Vase of Leftover Glass and Mirror ... 63

Project No. 14: Creating Colored Glass – by Yourself! ... 66

Summary ... 70

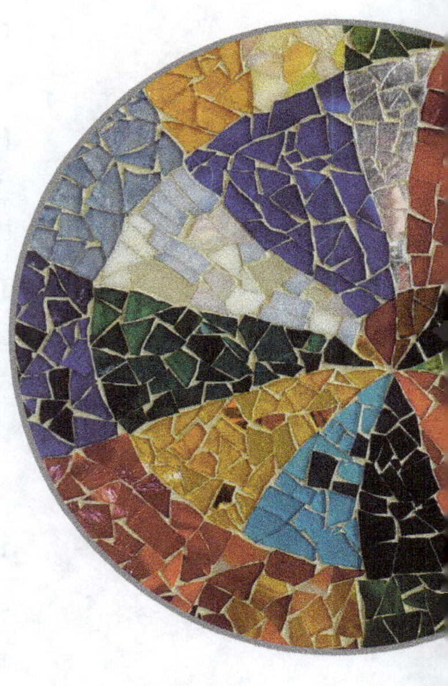

Introduction

I've always been fascinated by colored glass. It offers such a wealth of shades, blends, opacities and textures - like crafting a rainbow. For a flamboyance-enthusiast as me, walking into the colored glass section is like going into a candy store hungry!

I've encountered mosaics through the art of stained glass. I've dabbled in lampshades, pictures, boxes and more for several years, until I had my fill and decided to try something new.

I created a few pieces from leftover glass, and saw that they were good. From there, it was a short road to a new world, which mesmerizes me to this day.

I craft mosaics from just about any solid material, but glass, by far, produces the finest pieces.

It's a material which takes a little know-how. Not everyone is into this delicate work, and care should be taken not to get hurt, but once you learn the rules and tinker around, you'll discover its magic.

There's a myriad of techniques for working with glass – It can be done with the same method used for stained glass, cutting exact pieces and using grout to accentuate the spaces, or with special pliers for cutting various shapes.

In this book, we'll review a wide range of materials for mosaic work – From glass panels to store-bought tiles. Everything will be tackled here.

You will learn the basic techniques that do not require purchasing expensive gear (I'll get to that in the next book).

You will craft ornamental picture frames, but also functional items like trays and mirrors, in a clear and practical manner, step-by-step along with pictures and instructions.

The book is arranged progressively – From simple to more complex. Each project is presented clearly, with instructions and pictures plus helpful tips along the way.

At the end of the book there is a bonus for you. All the patterns that are showed, in this book, are available in a pdf file, for your use.

My name is Sigalit. This is my 7th book on mosaics. I love explaining and teaching things to others, and I welcome you to a close look at the rich world of glass mosaics, and to fall in love with the magic that is colored glass.

There is a bonus for you. All the patterns that are showed in this book, are available in a pdf file, for your use, at the end of the book (page 71).

Be creative and use your imagination,

Sigalit

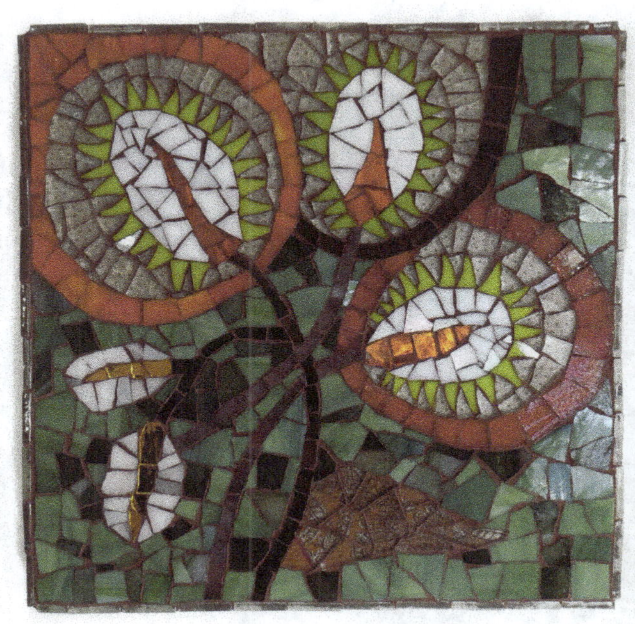

Why Glass?

Glass has numerous advantages in crafting mosaics:

Colorfulness – Glass panels come in every color imaginable, including shades mixed together to create magnificent blends

Glossy/Matte – Glass is sometimes clear and sometimes opaque, is mostly glossy but also comes in a variety processed to appear matte

Thickness – Glass isn't too thick to process

Cleaning – Adhesives come off glass very readily, which makes working with grout very easy

Price – Glass is more expensive than ceramics, however one can experiment with small glass works without too much expense: Buying leftover glass by weight, working with glass tiles or buying a large colorful piece when needed.

Tile size – One can process very small glass pieces to create delicate works, even jewelry.

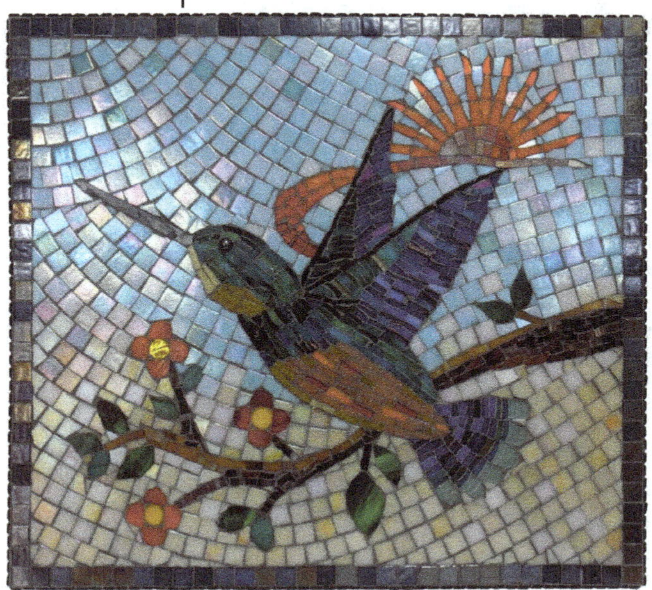

Cons:

Caution – Glass is very brittle and should be cut carefully to avoid injury. Use every necessary precaution when working. (See the dedicated chapter on page 9)

Glass Mosaic tools and equipment

First of all, prepare your working surface: Glass cutting needs a steady table. If you don't have one, use a heavy wooden board.

You will find links on some of the tools - you can press to see how the product looks.

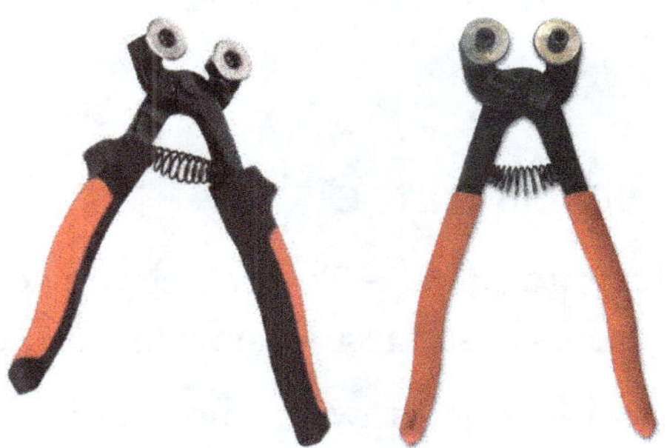

Wheeled glass nipper – for cutting glass in free shapes.

Glass cutter – For cutting straight lines or specific shapes. There are several kinds of cutters. The differences are in shape and price. I recommend you try and decide what cutter you like most. All cutters have a small wheel at the top - the difference is usually the handle configuration. For example:

<table>
<tr><td>Glass cutter
with a straight handle</td><td>Glass cutter
with plastic grip handle</td></tr>
<tr><td></td><td>(I love this one, just used to work with
this kind of cutter)</td></tr>
</table>

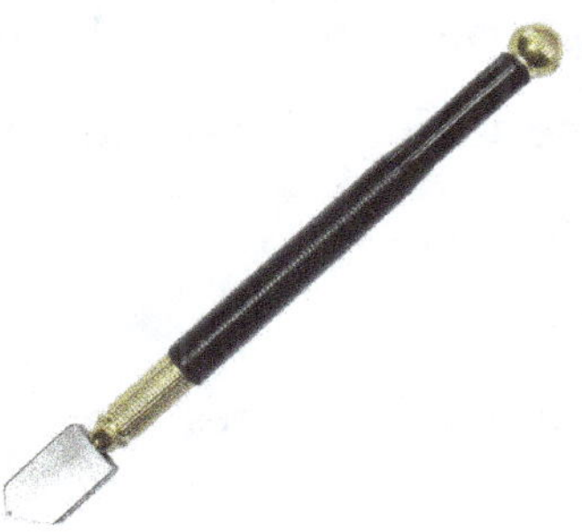

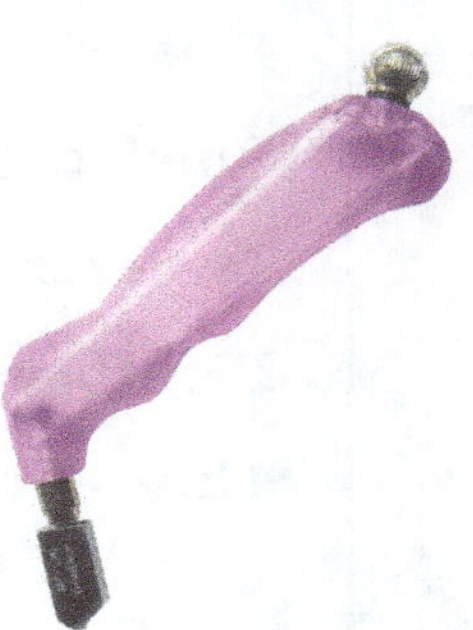

Pliers:

Breaking glass pliers / Running pliers – For breaking the glass after marking it with the glass cutter.

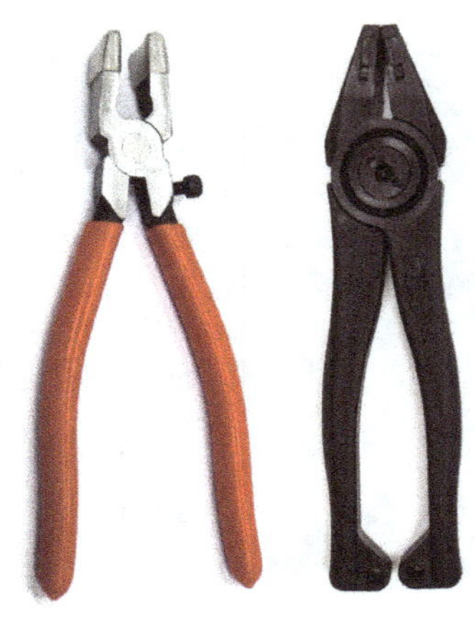

Breaker-Grozier Pliers - For breaking glass along score lines that can't be handled comfortably by hand. The cutter has 2 sides, one straight and one curved.

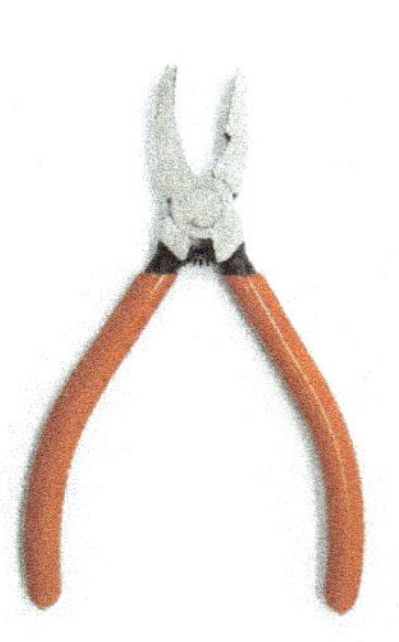

Preparation tools

Safety goggles – To protect your eyes from glass fragments. Use these when you cut the glass.

Pencil – For drawing the picture outline before painting.

Ruler – To mark straight lines.

T-Square – To help cutting the glass in straight lines.

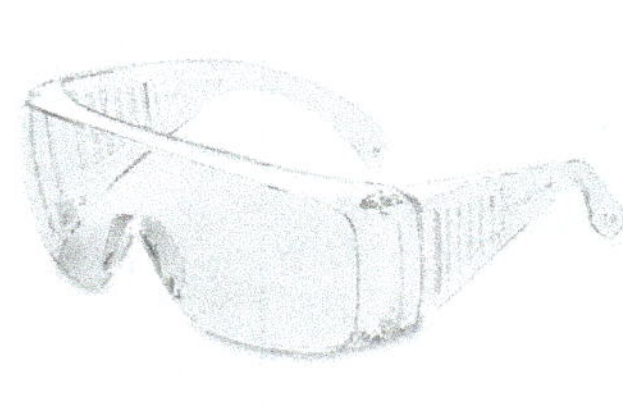

Glass paint marker – For marking shapes on the glass. It's better to have one black and one white or gold, for dark glass parts.

Latex gloves – To protect your hands from tiny bits of glass, scratches and dirt.

Carbon paper – To copy your design from paper onto your substrate material.

Plastic containers – For glue, water, cut glass or beads, and mixing colors

Small brush – For cleaning the surface of dust and small particles.

Tweezers – For placement of small parts.

Paintbrush – For adhesive application.

Thin screwdriver – For cleaning adhesive residue.

Grout – to fill the gaps between the tiles.

NOTE: There are different types of grout. Most of them come in powdered form, which you will need to mix with water according the manufacturer's instructions. Grout also comes in different colors, so choose the right color for your work. You can also mix acrylic paint into white grout to make your own custom colored grout, but if you do this, be sure that the final work is not exposed to the sun or water.

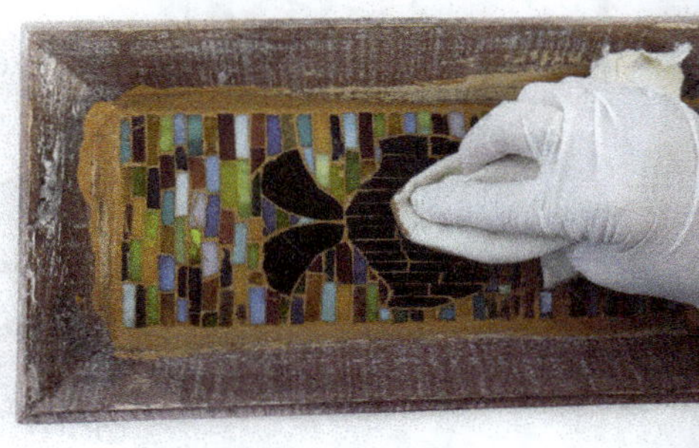

Working with the grout can be messy, so wear appropriate clothing and put on gloves before you begin.

Water – for making grout and cleaning.

Small squeegee – for gripping and putting the grout on straight surfaces.

Sponge or cotton rags – for grout cleaning.

Old newspapers – to put under your work to maintain a clean work surface.

Safety instructions

Safety is a very important topic in this book. Glass is sharp and small pieces can injure you, so be careful!

1. Always wear closed shoes. Don't walk barefoot on the floor where you are working. Small fragments will always land there.

2. Wear safety goggles and gloves when cutting glass.

3. Use a small brush to clean the working surface. Never clean the small glass fragments with your hands!

4. Vacuum the floor – better than moving dust around.

5. Keep young children and animals away.

6. Keep some Band-Aids nearby.

The Glass

Stained glass – comes in many colors and textures: Shiny, opaque, transparent, single color, a few shades of one color and even glass with multiple colors and shades.

The glass can be purchased as a square panel in different sizes, depending on your requirements. Price varies according to measurements, color (e.g. red is more expensive than green), type, texture and color blend (blended glass is more expensive than uniform color).

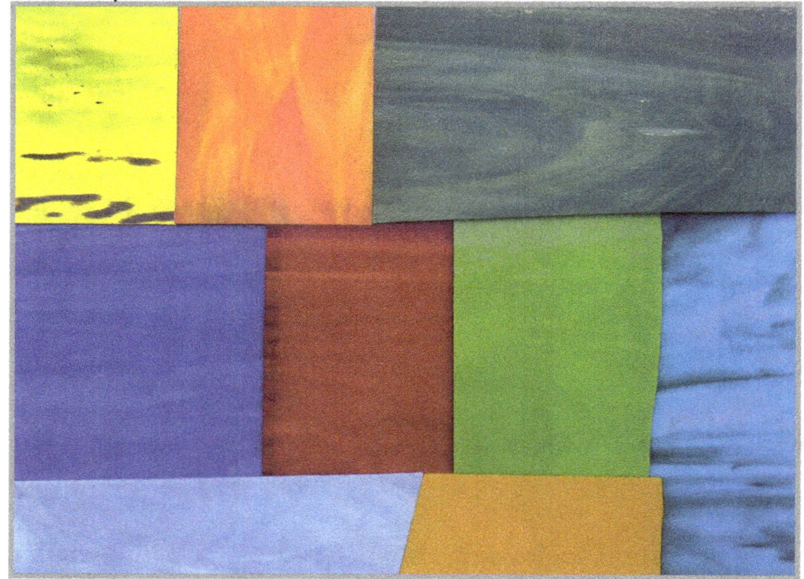

TIP: Try reaching out to stained glass artists and asking for leftover material or ask in stores selling glass – they sometimes sell it by weight. That's good enough to get started with.

Vitreous glass mosaic tiles – ready square glass tiles in a variety of sizes and colors. The glass can be glossy or grainy, clear or opaque, uniform or blended. Tile sizes start at 1 cm2 / 0.15in2, and you can buy sheets of sticker tiles or by weight.

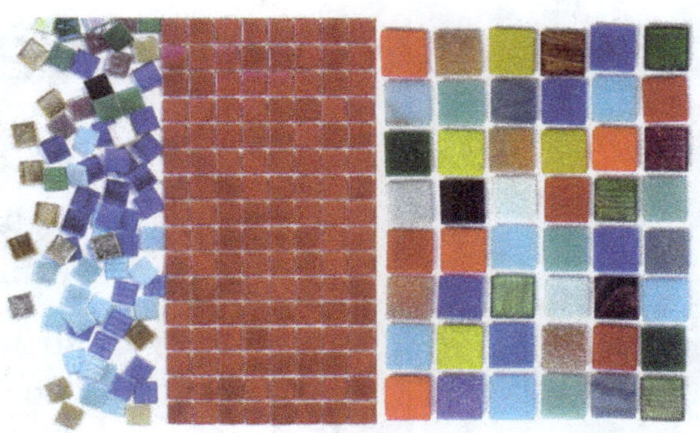

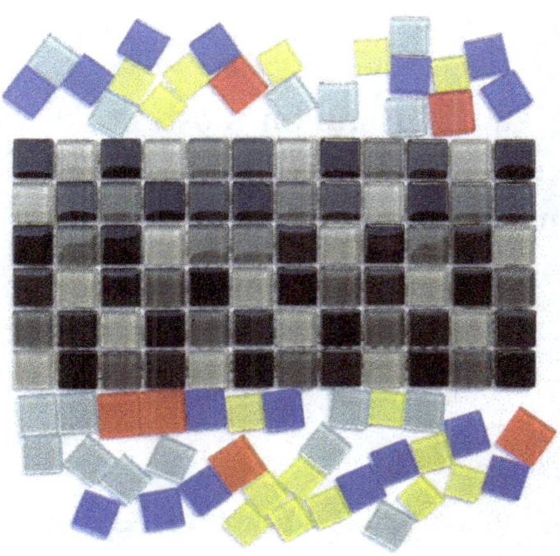

Clear glass tiles – These are tiles of clear glass glued to colored paper. The paper is reflected outward, giving the tile its color.

Mirrors – Mirror tiles blend nicely into glass mosaics and create a pleasing effect. The mirror serves as an additional raw material and can be cut with the same techniques used for colored glass.

Smalti – Colored glass chunks with very vivid colors. We'll leave the Smalti to more advanced installments; the book will not cover this material.

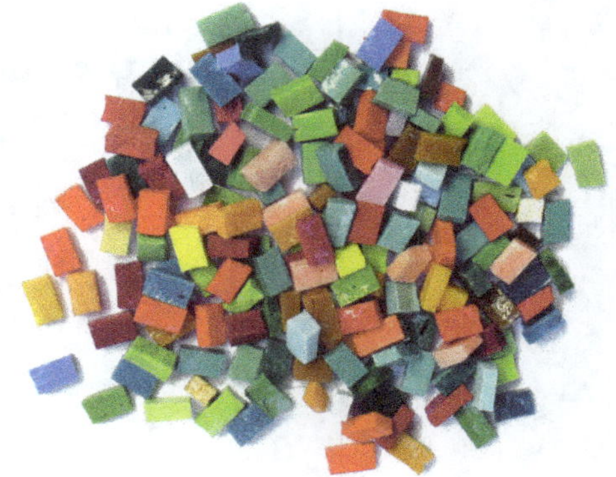

Adhesives

For proper use of glue, always read the manufacturer's instructions. Use the glue that is most comfortable for you to work with.

Note: The glue should be compatible with the type of surface you're crafting and to the work's final placement: If you intend to hang the piece outdoors, pick weather-resistant glue, such as tile adhesive. If the piece will remain indoors, you can opt for white glue, which is more convenient to use.

PVA white glue – This glue is useful for most mosaic works, especially wooden surfaces. I recommend first sampling on a small segment to verify its strength. There are various kinds of white glue, with varying levels of adhesiveness.

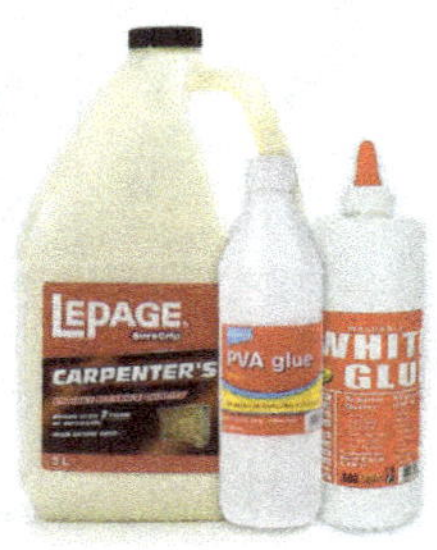

Glass glue – For pasting onto a glass substrate (like E6000)

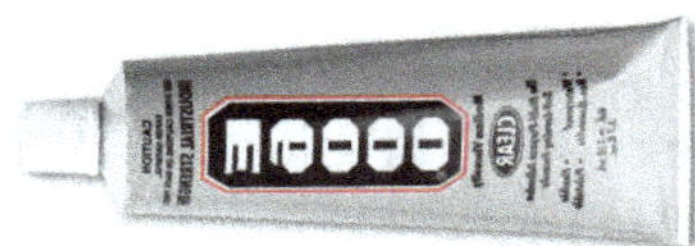

Mosaic tile adhesive – For pasting onto metal, clay or ceramic pots

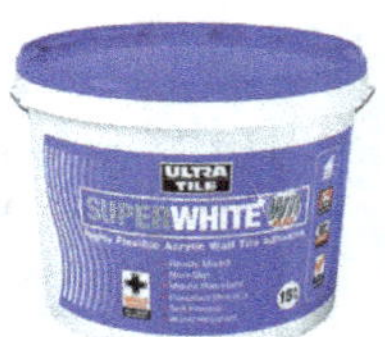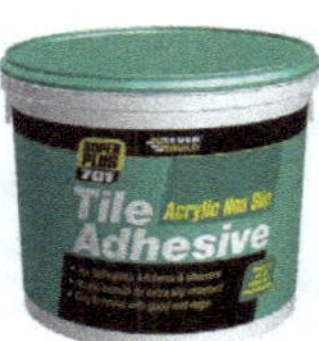

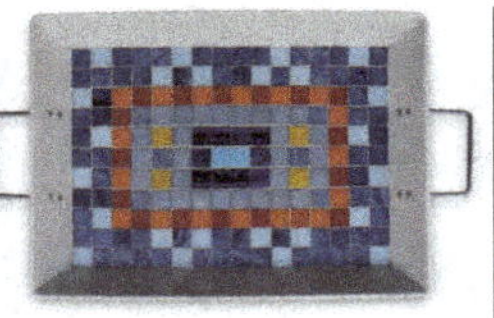

Project No. 1: Colorful Tile Tray

The easiest way to work with glass is using colored tiles. During their first lesson many of my students insist on using just the tiles and are wary of using the cutter. It may seem like very simple work, but I greatly enjoy it – mixing colors and patterns, and handling the material without worrying about scrapes and cuts. If you work properly, the result will be a shiny, smooth tray which you can gift or use to serve coffee to your guests on every chance you get!

In this work, I've used a light gray metal tray. The pattern fits the size I used, but naturally you can adjust it to whatever you use.

Materials:

Metal or wooden tray (not plastic), inner size 32 x 22 cm / 12.6"x8.66"

2 cm vitreous glass mosaic tiles in 8 colors: Dark blue, blue, 2 shades of light blue, gray, yellow, red and orange

PVA white glue

Paintbrush

Gray Grout

Grout equipment: Mixing bowl, water, a wooden stick, rags, gloves

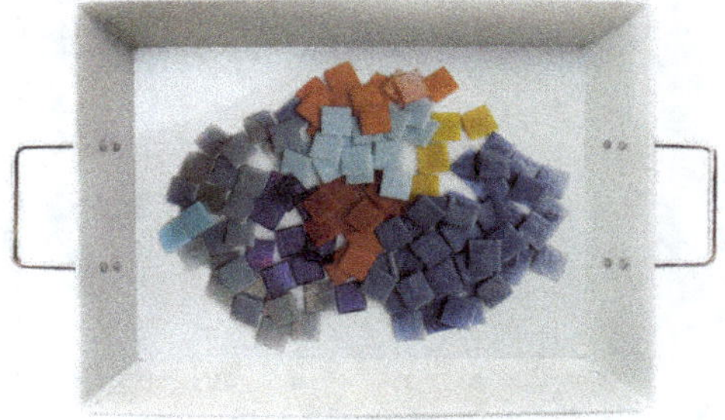

1 We begin gluing from the outside frame inward. Before you begin, make sure that the pattern fits inside the tray and the glass tiles don't have too much space between them. That way, you won't need to copy the pattern onto the tray, but rather follow the instructional images and glue accordingly.

2 Using a fine brush, spread glue on the tray's outer rim and glue two lines of blue and azure tiles, according to the pattern. Naturally, you can use other techniques, such as spreading a thin layer of glue on the back of the tile and place it. Make sure that the smooth, glossy side of the glass is pointing upward.

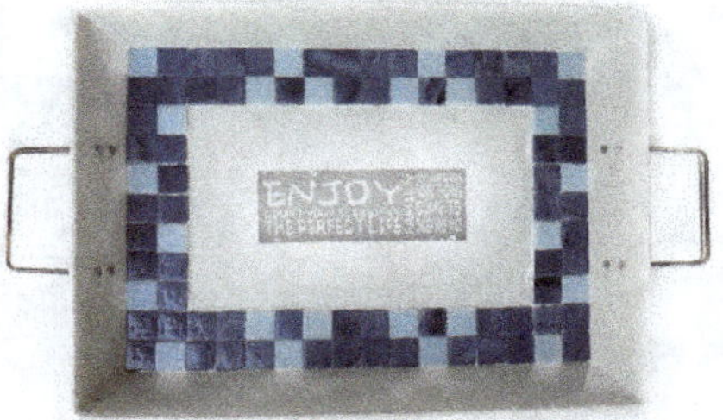

3 Third row – alternating orange and red. Take care to keeping the row straight

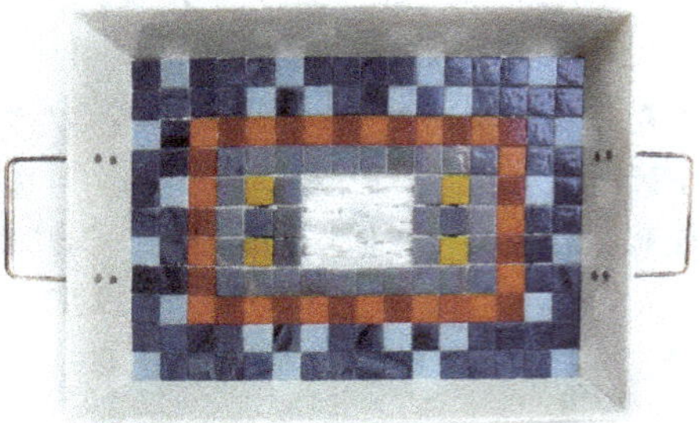

4 Then, glossy gray-azure glass tiles with a yellow tile for accentuation.

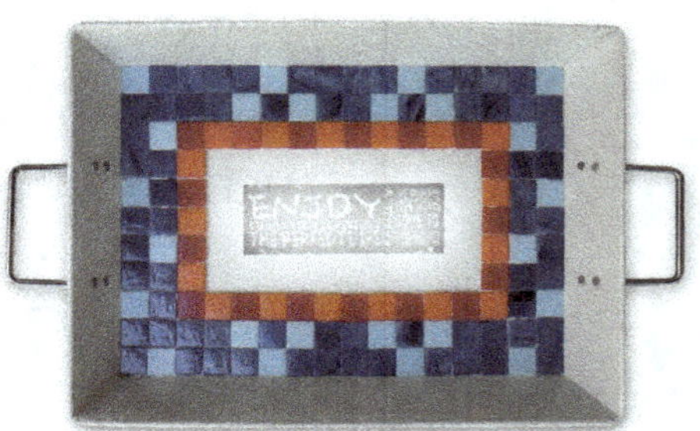

5 Complete the tray by gluing a blue rectangle with two azure tiles. Leave the tray to dry for at least one day.

6 Prepare the grout according to the stages below, dry and polish the tray.

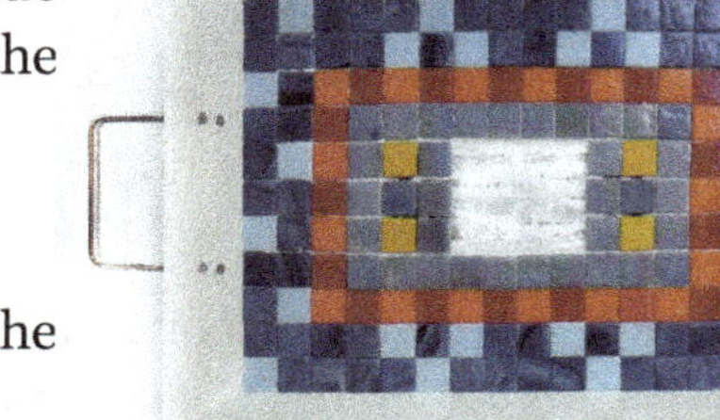

Applying a grout - step by step:

1 Wear a dust mask to protect your face and wear rubber gloves.

2 Cover the working surface with old newspapers.

3 Put a few tablespoons of grout of the desired color in a plastic bowl (possibly the tray's color). If there's not enough grout in the mix —add grout and water in the same bowl.

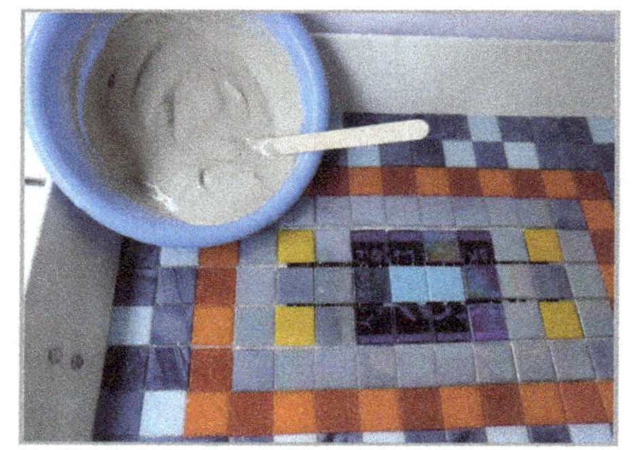

4 Pour water into the grout bowl. Mix with a wooden stick until the texture becomes creamy. Note the manufacturer's instructions.

5 Apply the grout: Pour some grout on the tray. Use a small squeegee or cake scraper to spread the grout until it fills in every slot and hole.

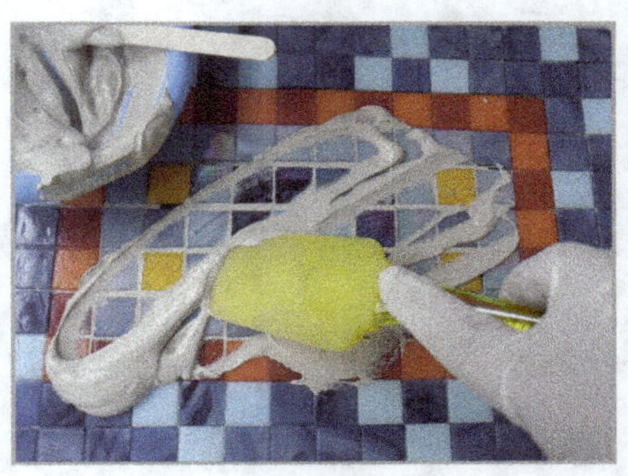

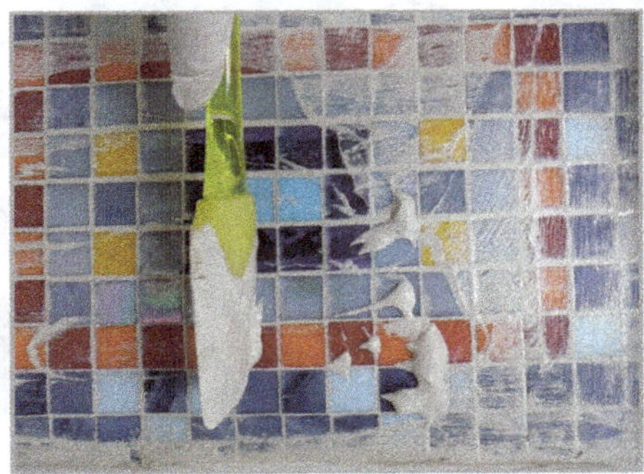

6 When the piece is covered in grout, use a squeegee or cake scraper to remove excess.

7 Wait a few minutes until the grout starts to dry, and begin cleaning: Douse the surface using a clean cotton rag or a sponge. Use a wet and then dry rag several times until the piece is clean.

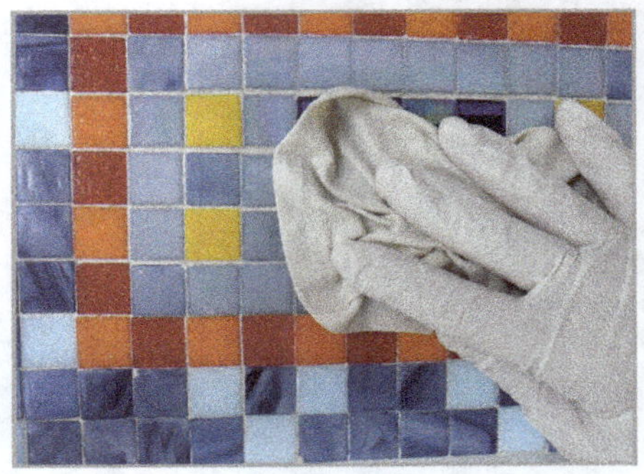

8 IMPORTANT: Make sure to wet the work. Wetting the grout makes it harder and prevents cracks. Don't skip this step!

9 If "holes" show up after cleaning, fill them with grout, leave to dry and clean until you get a smooth, clean result.

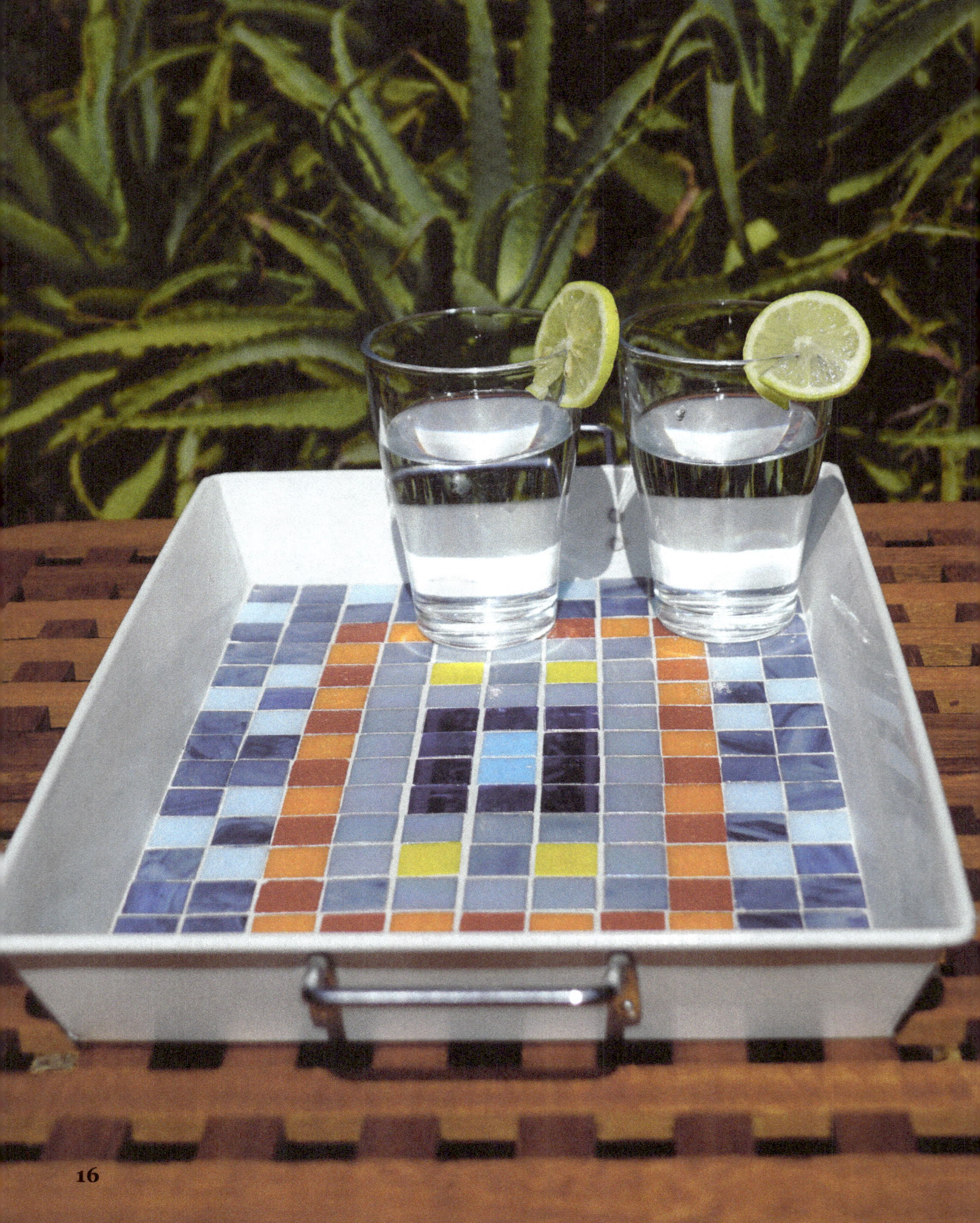

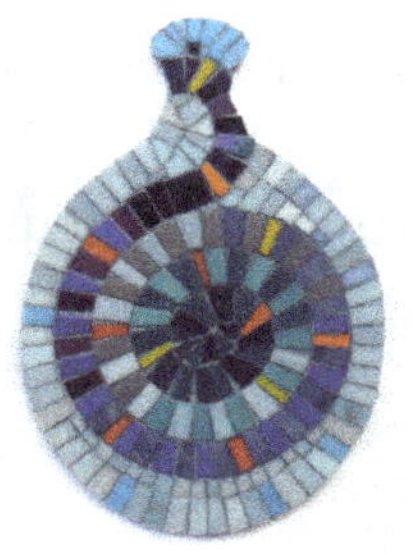

Project No. 2: Spiral

Glass tiles can be used in several ways – obviously, you can leave them whole, but you can also cut them to stripes, smaller squares or triangles.

This spiral is composed solely of cut tiles. Begin working from the inside out, first with two colors, then alternating only one of the colors, and so on. Between the colors, mix in thin strips of yellow and orange, to make the piece more vivid. The spiral is set on a paddle-shaped wooden surface with a hole in the handle to hang it with, but can also be created on a rectangular or circular surface.

Materials:

A paddle-shaped wooden surface with a handle, approximately 19 cm / 7.5" wide

Vitreous glass tiles in the following shades: Azure, dark green, gray, turquoise, orange, several shades of blue, and a few orange and yellow tiles

PVA white glue

Paintbrush

Gray Grout

Grout Equipment: Mixing bowl, water, a wooden stick, rags, gloves

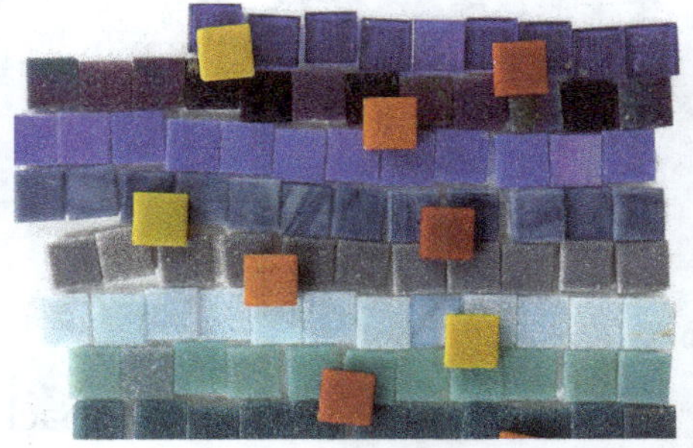

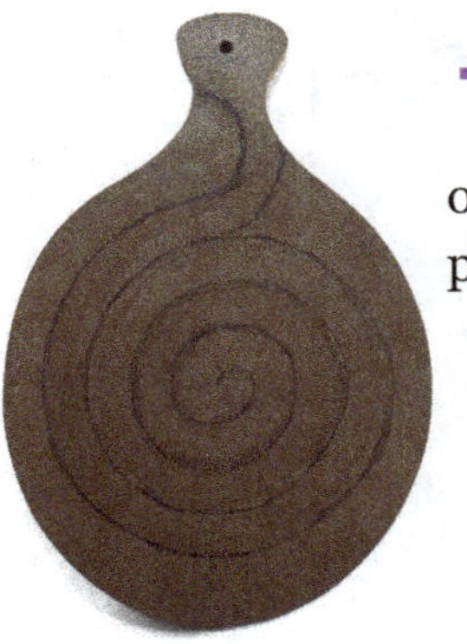

1 Copy the spiral pattern onto the wooden surface using a pencil and tracing paper.

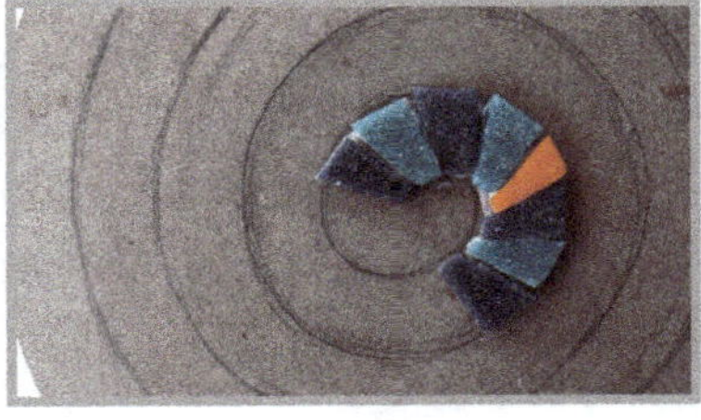

2 Cut tiles in two shades of dark green into a slightly diagonal shape (see instructions on cutting the tiles below). Begin at the center in the first spot you can fit the height of a tile in, according to the picture. We'll complete the rest later. Mix a thin piece of orange tile between the greens.

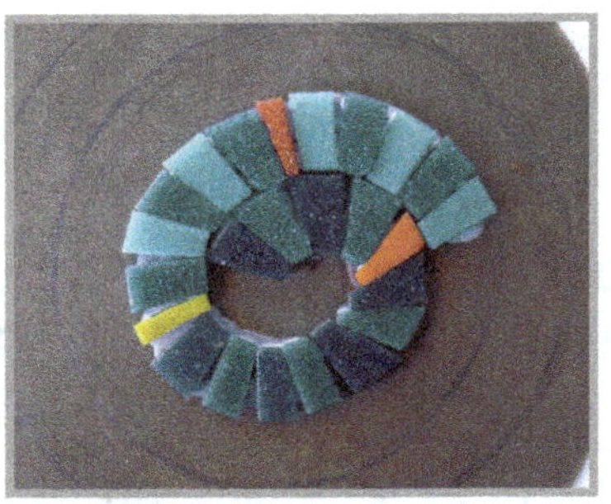

3 Add the third color, turquoise – each time, we'll pass on the first color and add another instead. Occasionally we will throw in a narrow strip of orange or yellow. Now you can cut the tiles in two with straight edges, at the center of each tile.

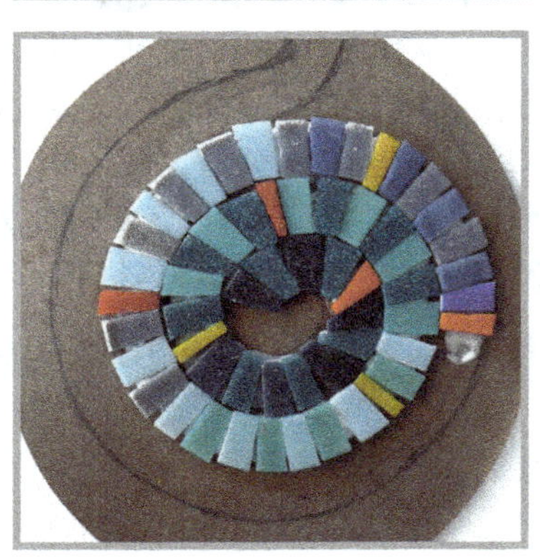

4 Continue adding colors. The image shows the azure, gray and blue which come after the turquoise.

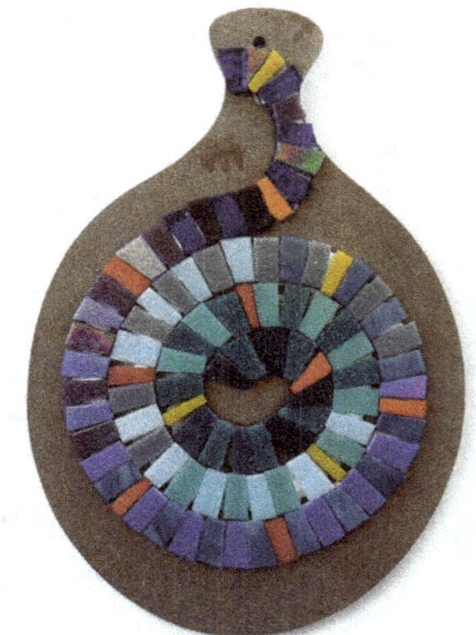

5 Complete the spiral all the way to the top by gluing dark blue tiles. Match the size of the cut shape to its placement.

6 Filling in the center: Cut triangles and glue them in a circular fashion to complete the spiral center.

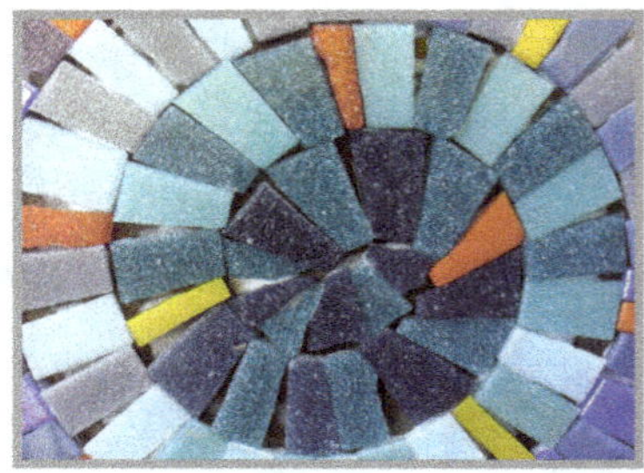

7 For the background, cut azure tiles in two. If you're left with a gap, fill it with small pieces. It's important to first glue the tiles to the edges of the surface before filling the center, in order to give the work a nice finish.

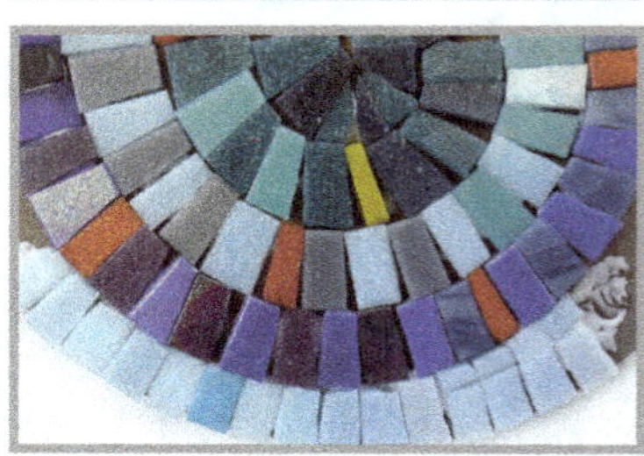

8 Fill in all the background pieces in this manner. The surface I chose has a hole in its handle for hanging. On the edge of the handle, glue dark azure cut tiles, fitting each piece in its place. Leave to dry for 24 hours.

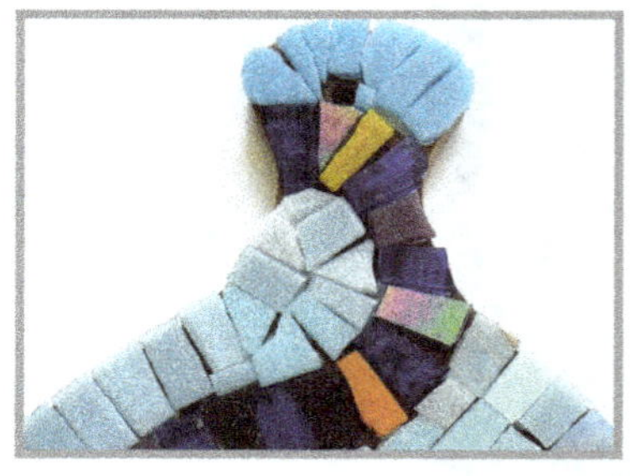

Cutting glass tiles:

In order to cut the glass tiles, we'll use a nipper. Hold the instrument in your dominant hand and grab the glass tile at its center. Pay attention to the instrument's angle relative to the tile. The cut will follow the angle you hold it in – either straight or diagonal.

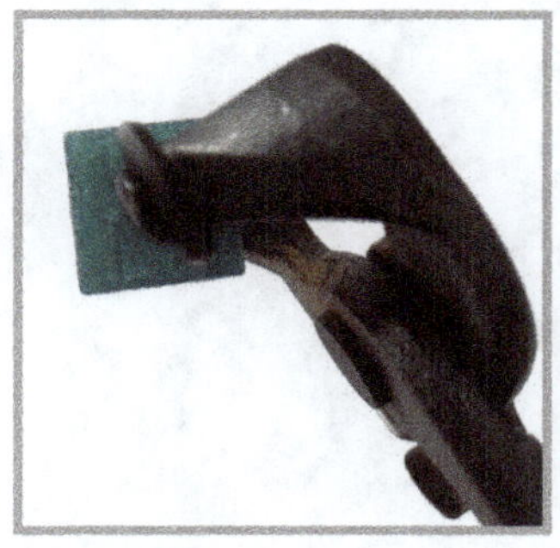

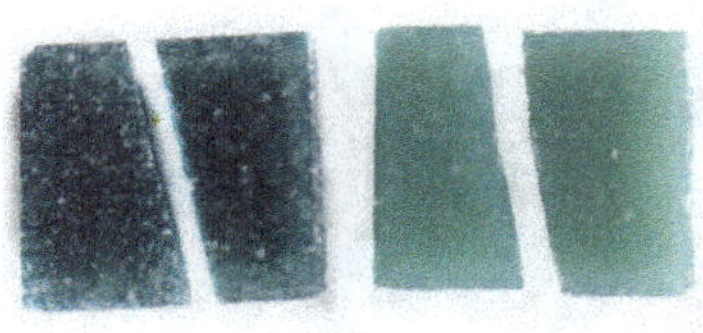

Diagonal cuts are used for creating circular patterns, making the spaces between the pieces smaller.

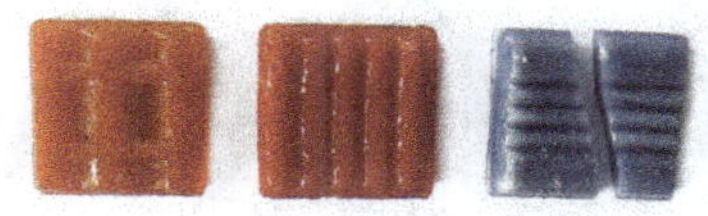

TIP: Notice the other side of the tile – It's usually rough in order to give the glue more traction. Try to cut perpendicular to the ribbing – otherwise, the cut will follow one of the ribs, making it harder to control the width of the cut.

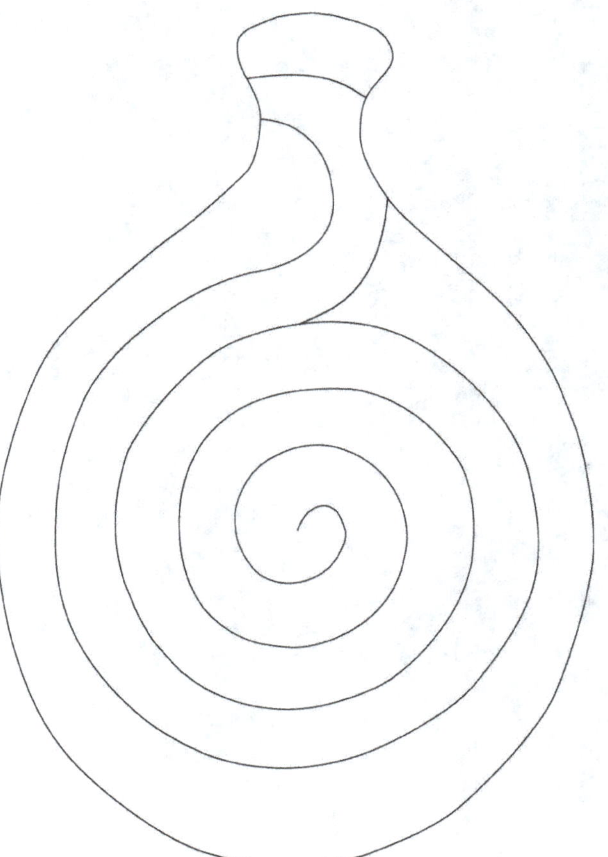

Pattern for the Spiral:
Enlarge on a photocopier by 160% for a full size design

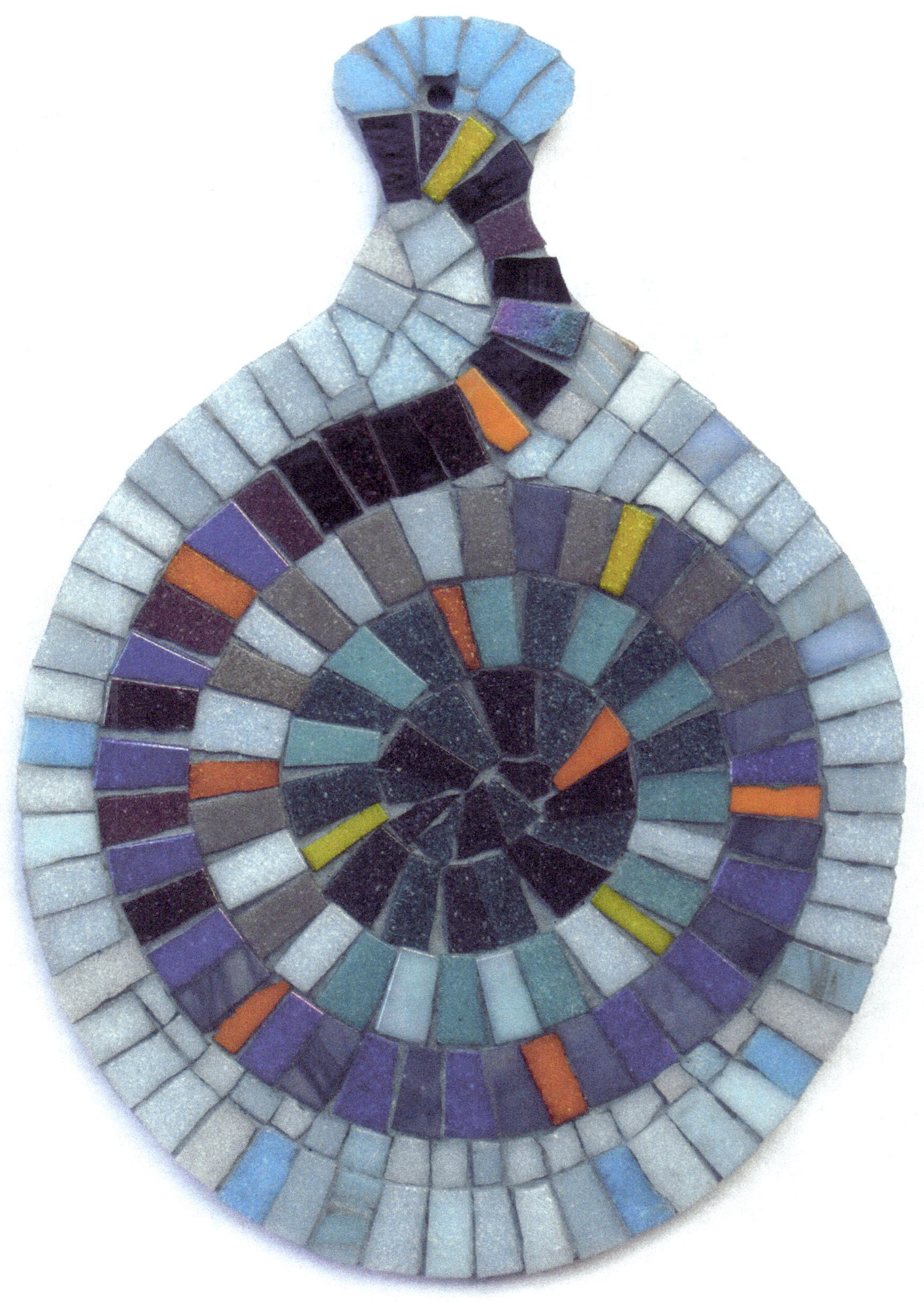

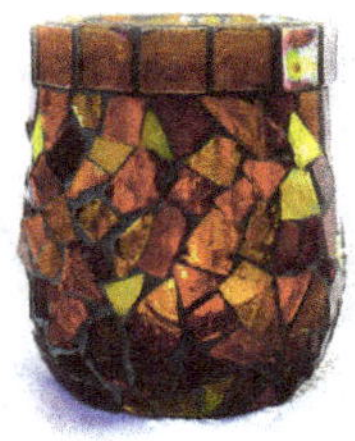

Project No. 3: Candle Holder

I love having lit candles around the house, especially on cold, stormy evenings. I have a collection of candle holders which decorate the house, but it's much more fun to make one yourself and enjoy the candle light as well as the colors it projects through the glass.

This piece is great as a gift – it's simple to make, and can be crafted with any colored glass you have and on any small, smooth glass receptacle you can find. For gluing the glass, I used an appropriate glass adhesive. Make sure you stick to the instructions – Since gluing the glass onto the receptacle is performed vertically and pieces tend to slide downward if glued incorrectly.

Materials:

A small glass receptacle (should be smooth and bump-free), I used 9.5 cm / 3.7" tall

Red/orange glass tiles

Red, orange and yellow glass

Glass adhesive (I used E-6000)

Nipper

Gloves

Plastic stick

Black grout

Grout Equipment: mixing bowl, water, a wooden stick, rags, gloves

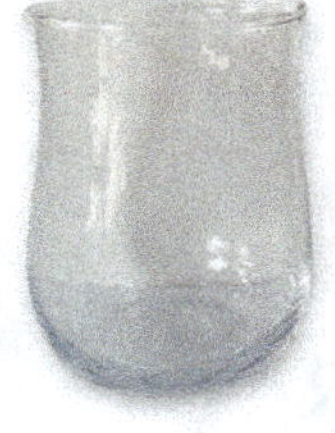
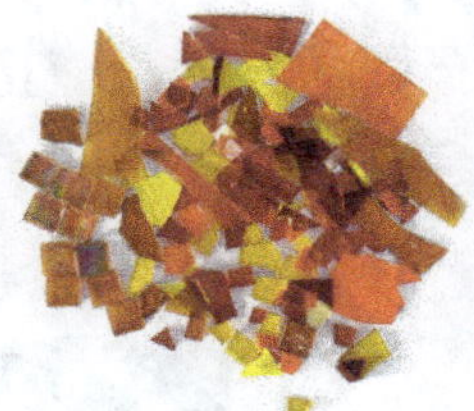

1 Cut the glass tiles using the nipper in shades of red, orange and yellow into small, random shapes. Smaller pieces will make working with the receptacle's round shape easier (see instructions on cutting the glass below)

2 Wear gloves – Working with glass adhesive should always be done with gloves.

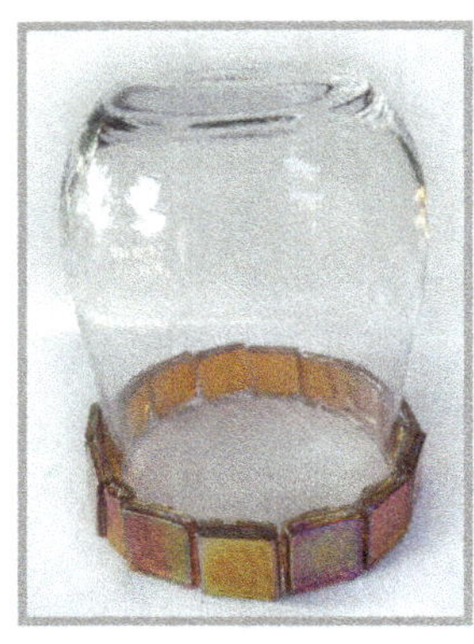

3 First, glue the tiles to create the receptacle's rim. They should be glued with tiny spaces and care should be taken so that they don't overlap. Using a wooden stick, rub some glue onto the back of each tile and glue it to the rim. To keep the row of tiles leveled, turn the receptacle upside down and align the tiles with your work surface. This will block the tiles from sliding down.

4 Glue the glass tiles you've cut onto the receptacle while maintaining small gaps. Keep a straight line at the finish for a more pleasing look.

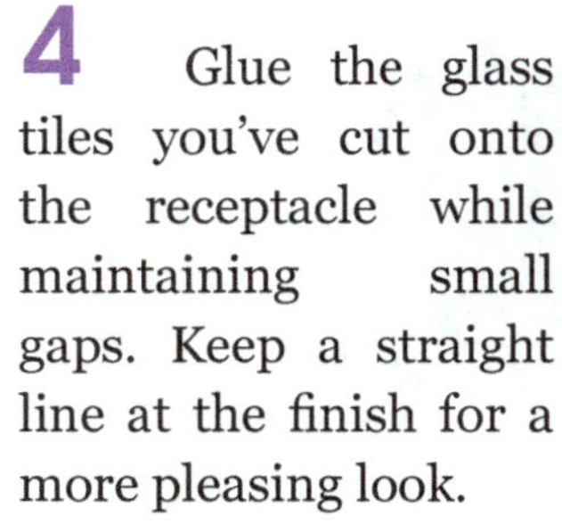

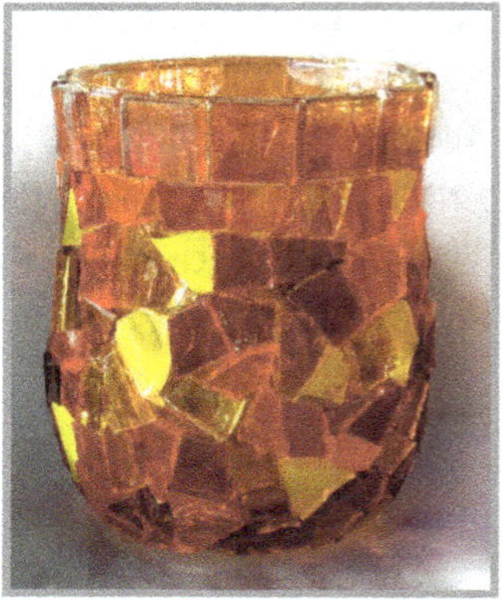

5 Leave to dry for 24 hours.

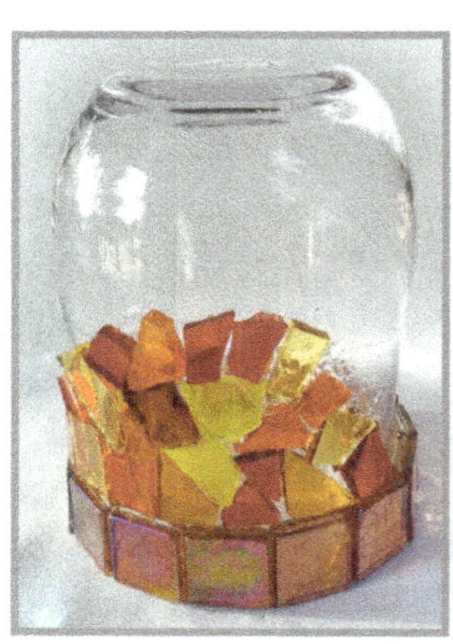

6 Prepare black grout according to manufacturer's instructions.

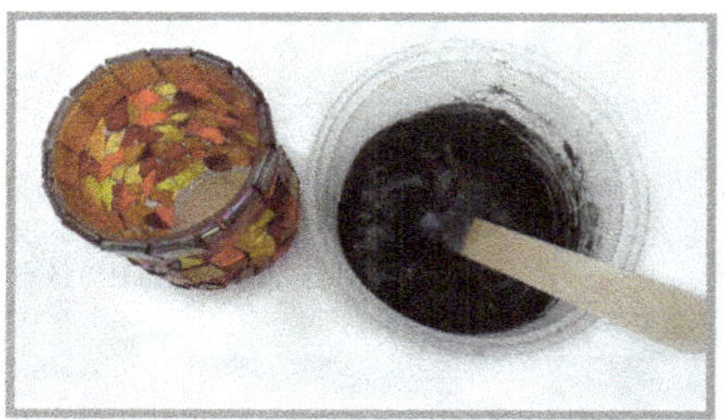

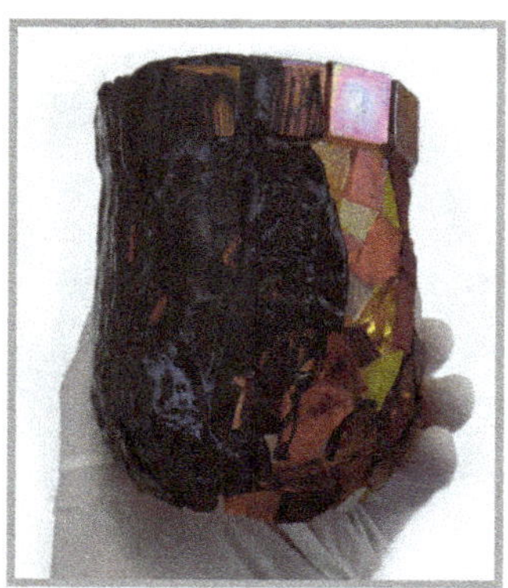

7 Hold the glass receptacle in one hand and spread the grout over all the tiles using a wood stick.

8 Clean thoroughly and polish with a wet rag.

9 Now you can insert a candle into the holder and enjoy its colorful glow.

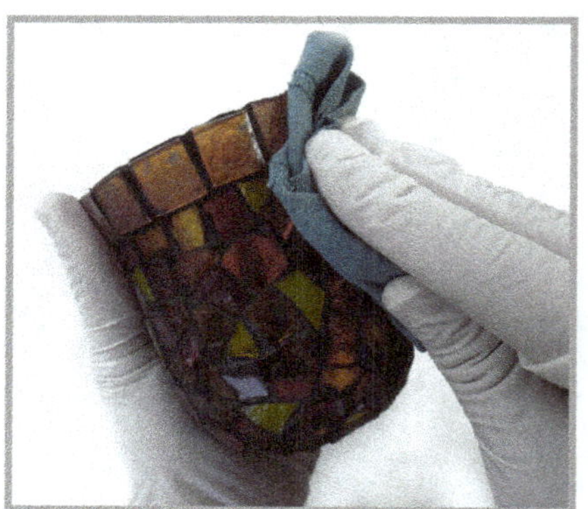

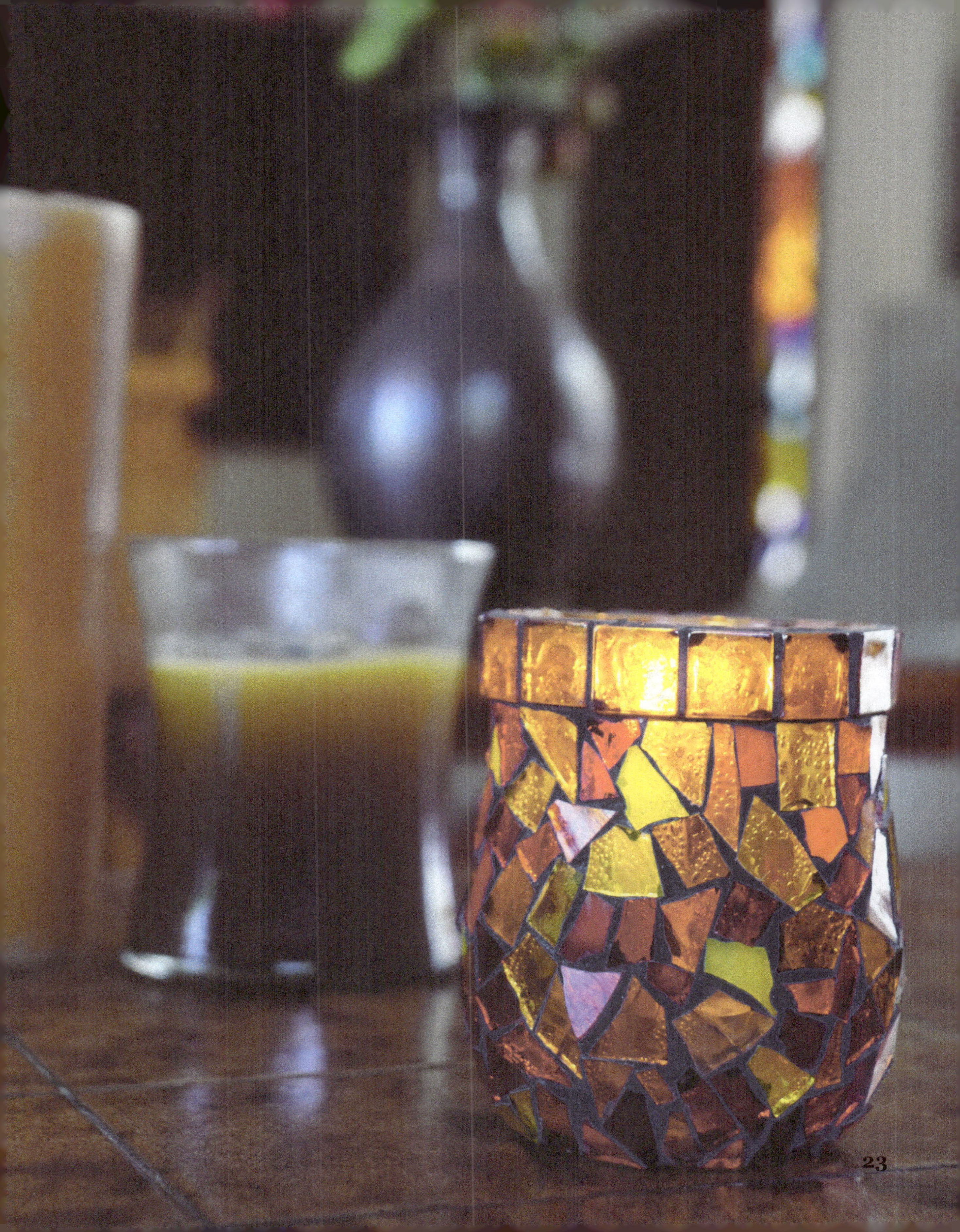

Cutting Glass with a Nipper

Glass can be cut in a variety of methods, each providing a different effect for our mosaic. In this book you will find several glass mosaic works, each using a different type of cut:

- Cutting straight lines with a special glass cutter (page 33)

- Cutting exact shapes using the glass cutter – a technique borrowed from stained glass making

- Using the nipper to cut triangles, thin stripes or various random shapes.

The simplest and fastest way to cut glass is **using the nipper:**

Hold the glass nipper with your dominant hand by its bottom element. Use your other hand to hold the glass. Place the glass between the wheels and cut away. The shape you'll get depends on the angle and manner in which you hold the glass. Over time, you'll learn to control the nipper grip and succeed in creating whatever shape you like.

When cutting with the nipper, take into account that the cut won't necessarily be straight like you would get when cutting with a ruler, but rather rounded.

In order to cut relatively straight lines, make sure you hold the nipper with a right angle to the glass.

TIP: When cutting glass, tiny pieces could shoot off in any direction. It's a good idea to cut inside a deep bowl (a plastic box would do). You'd be wise to use gloves to avoid scrapes and cuts.

In order to cut a triangle shape, hold the nipper in an angle and cut to the desired shape.

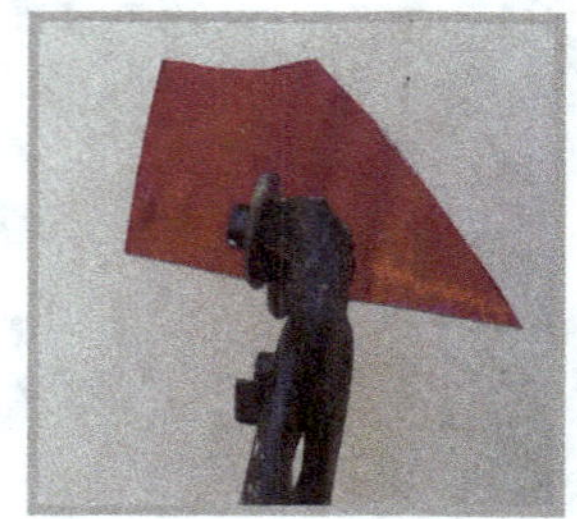

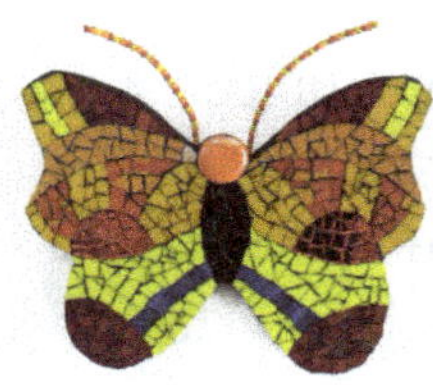

Project No. 4: Butterfly

This piece is nice in any room of the house. It's light and colorful. The glass is glued on wood. You can cut the butterfly shape according to the pattern herein using a saw, or buy it readymade in hobby and craft shops. You may also add antennas made from wire, onto which you can string colorful beads, and attach a hanger on the back.

If you don't have the option of sawing yourself, you can copy the pattern to the center of a 30 cm x 30 cm or 11" x 11" wooden board, and color the background or fill it with white mosaic tiles.

The colored glasses will be cut using the nipper, and the gluing will be in a jigsaw style – tightly fitting the pieces and matching their shapes as best as you can.

Follow safety instructions – put gloves on and watch for glass shrapnel flying off to undesired areas.

You can change the colors to any colorful mix you like. It would be rather nice to see several adjacent pieces of the same shape with different colors.

Materials:

A plywood butterfly 6-8 mm (0.23"-0.31") thick, 9.5" / 24 cm wide

Glass in shades of red, 3 shades of orange, 2 shades of yellow, blue and black

A large orange nugget

Tracing paper

Pencil

Strong white glue

Brush

Nipper

Tweezers

Plastic boxes

Black Grout

Grout Equipment: Mixing bowl, water, a wooden stick, rags, gloves

If you want to add antennas: Wire and small colorful beads

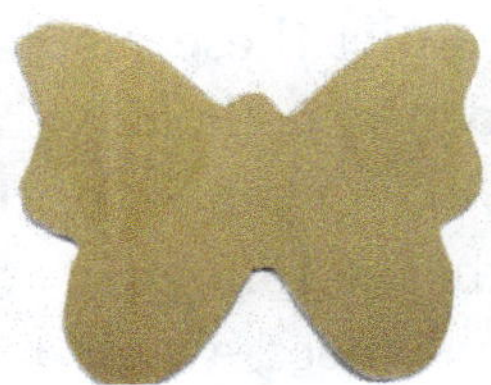

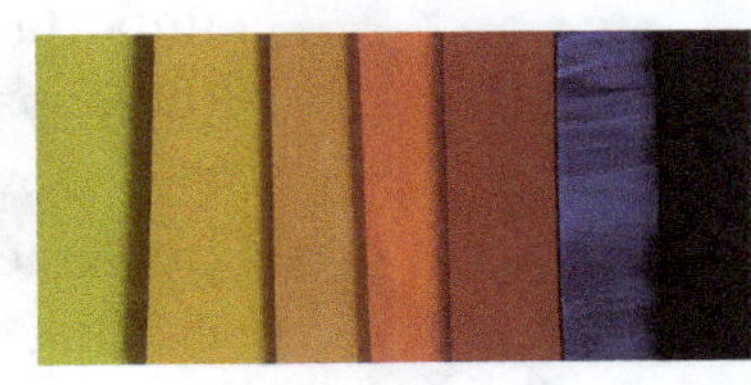

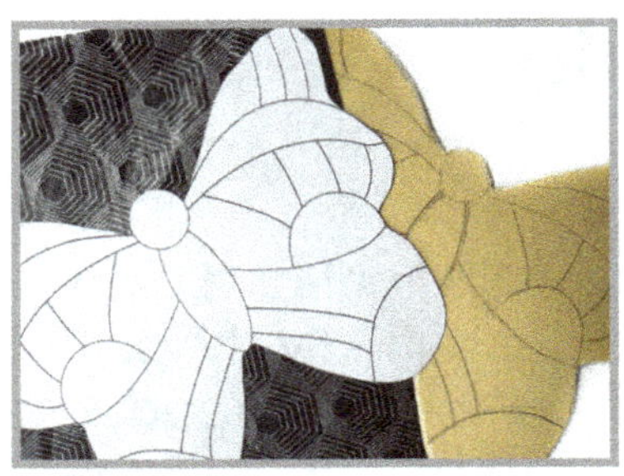

1 Print the butterfly pattern and copy to the wood with tracing paper.

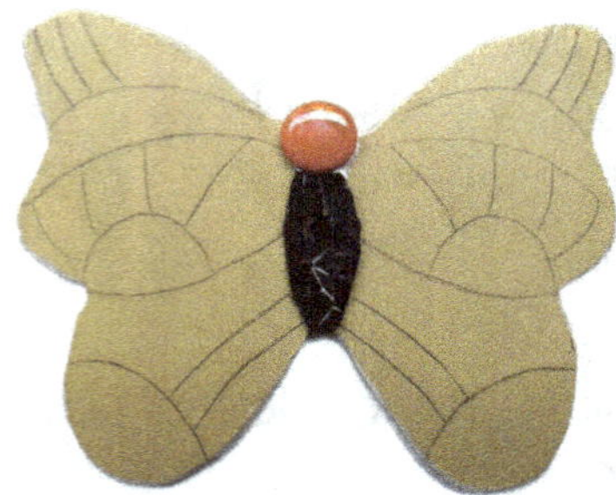

2 Glue the nugget to its place as the butterfly's head. Cut black glass into small random pieces. These will compose the butterfly's body. Glue in place with white glue while keeping the edge as smooth as possible with minimal gaps between the pieces.

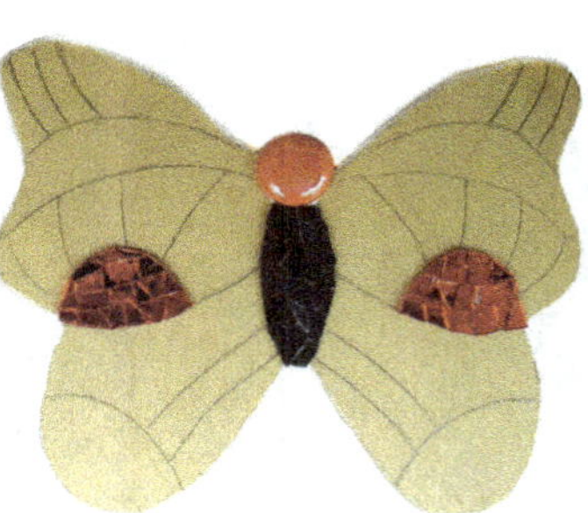

3 Top wings: Start from the lower half-circle, and glue vivid orange glass (I used a mirror-like orange). You can use the tweezers to place the tinier pieces.

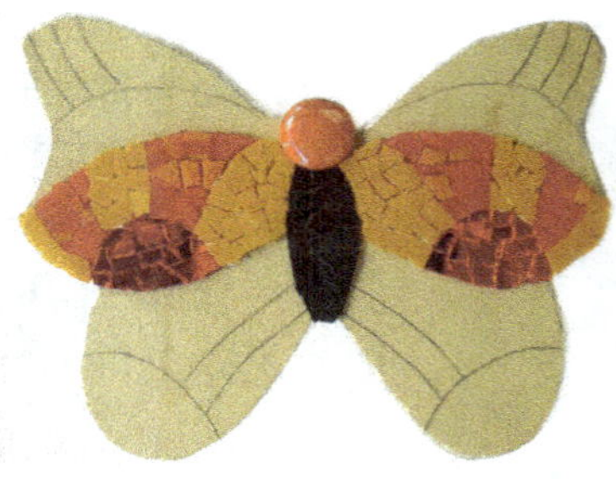

4 Cut glass in orange and amber-yellow, and glue on top of the half-circle as shown in the image.

5 Add a horizontal stripe in a different shade of orange.

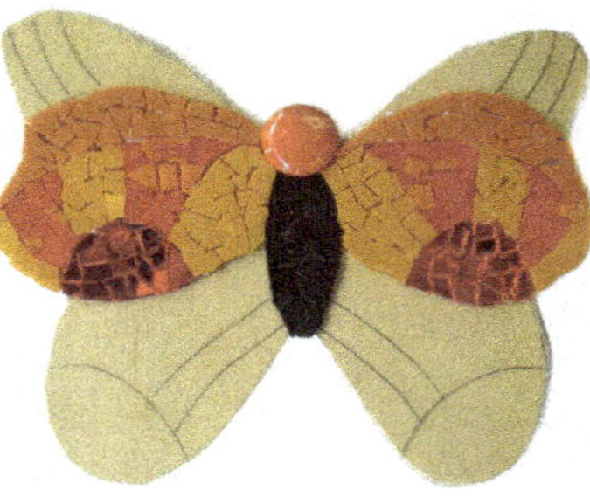

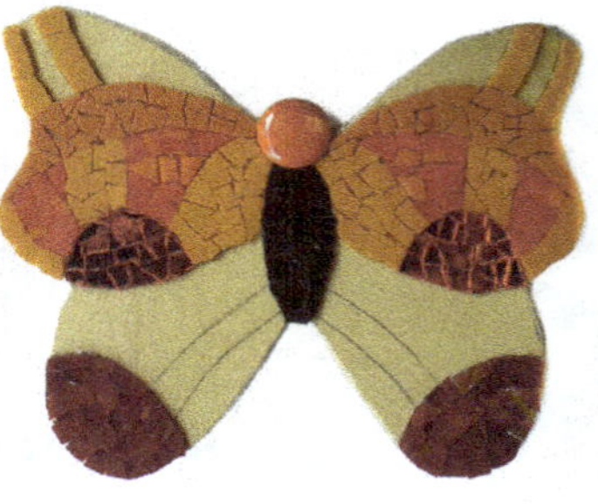

6 The top part of the butterfly will be glued in two stages: First, cut amber-yellow glass in shapes that will fit the longitudinal stripes. It's important to let these pieces dry before filling the gaps between them; otherwise everything will move out of place. In the meantime, you can glue the bottom part of the butterfly with small pieces of red glass. Cutting small pieces would make it easier to fit each one in its place.

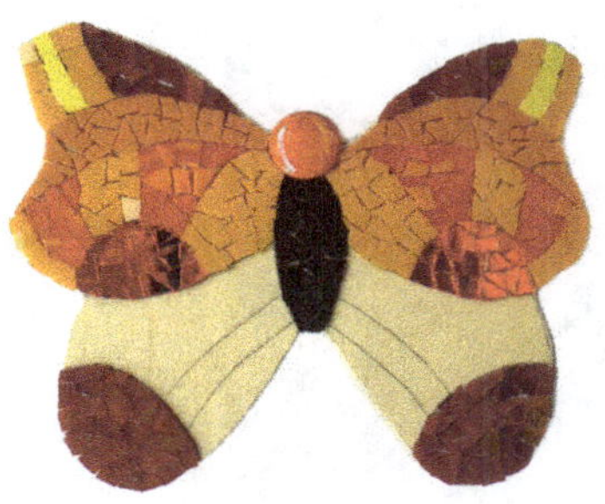

7 Now you can continue gluing the top. Stick yellow glass in the gap between the amber-yellow stripes. Here as well, it's important to match the shape of the glass to produce a neat stripe. Glue red glass in the remaining part.

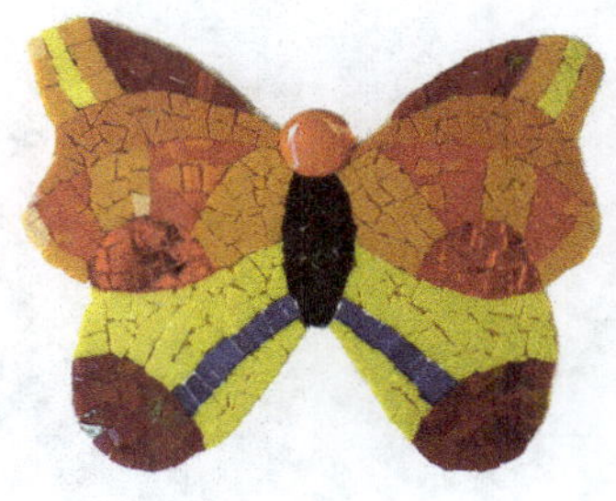

8 At the bottom of the butterfly, cut blue glass into longitudinal stripes and glue on the center stripe. Glue random yellow pieces on the remaining parts.

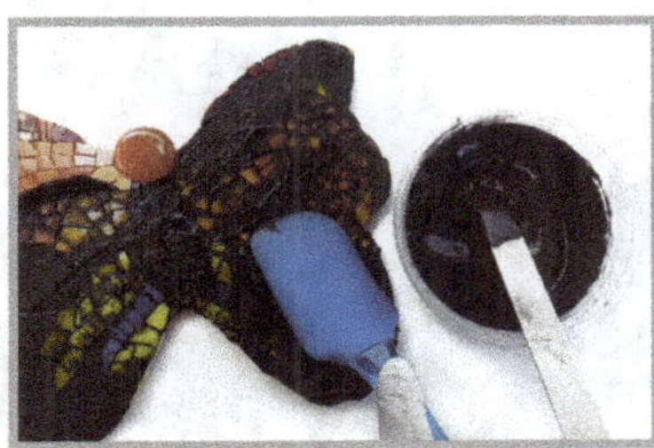

9 Leave to dry for 24 hours.
Prepare black grout according to instructions and apply to the butterfly. When done, clean thoroughly and polish with a wet rag.

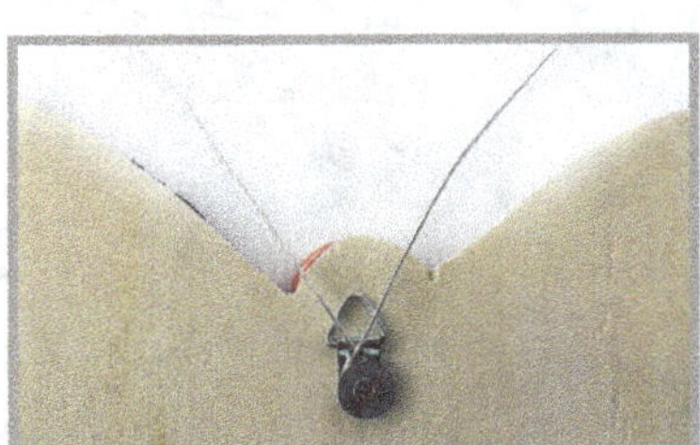

10 Now is the time to add a hanger and if you want antennas: Turn the butterfly over and using a pencil, mark the spot for the hanger. Place the hanger and loosely screw it in. Grab a wire, fold in half and twist around the screw, below the hanger. Continue inserting the screw all the way.

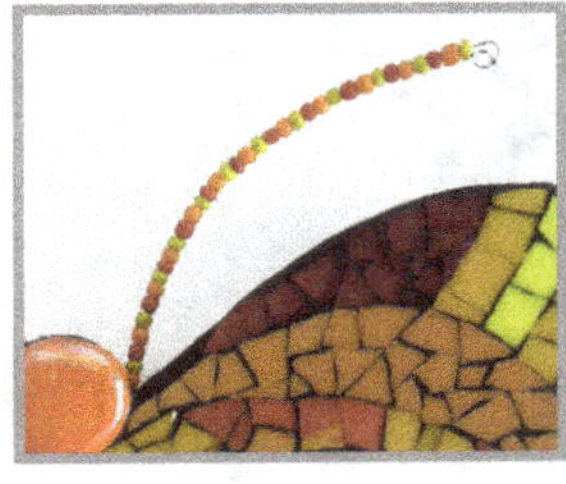

11 Thread the wires with colorful beads. When done, twist the wire tips several times with pliers to keep the beads from coming off.

Pattern for the Butterfly:
Enlarge on a photocopier by 320% for a full size design

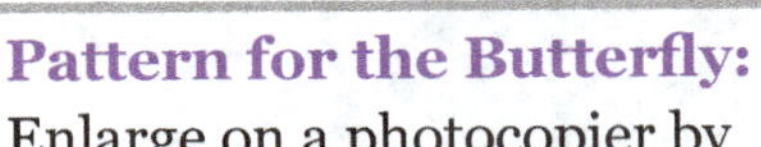

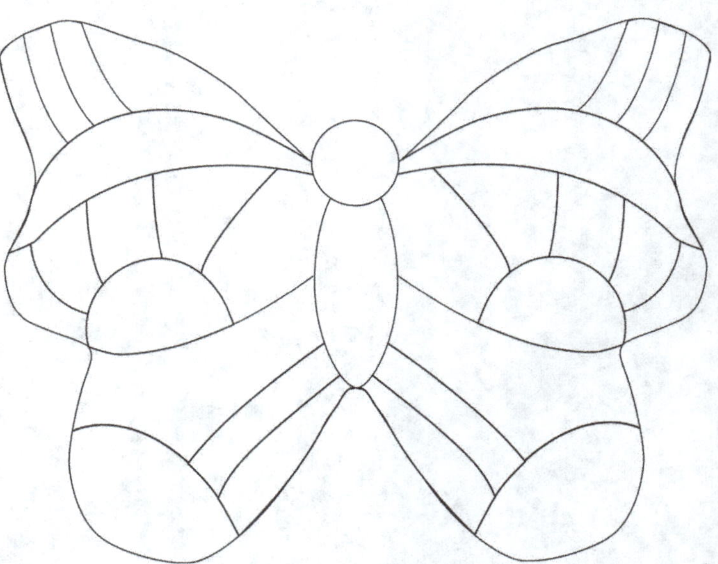

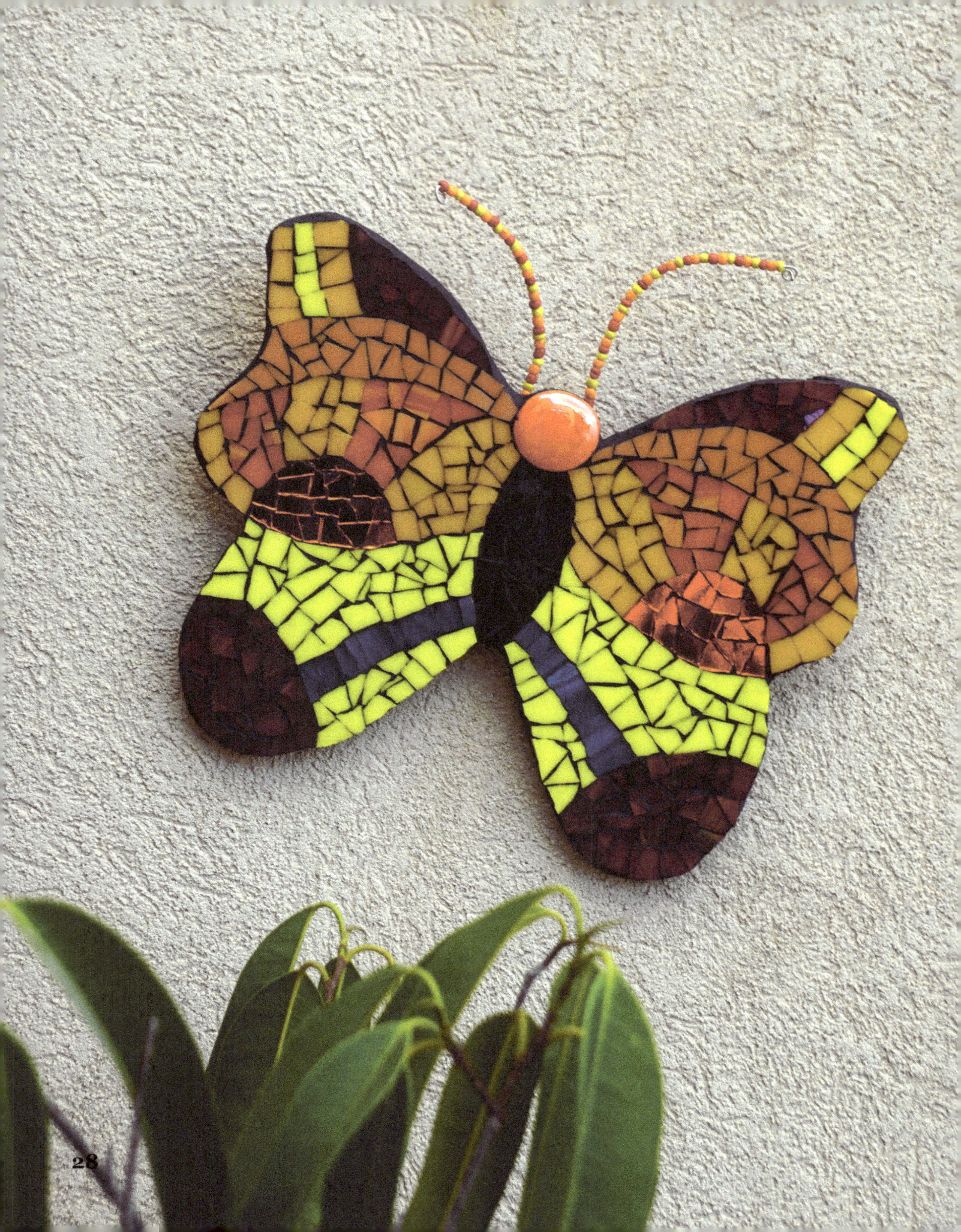

Gluing Glass

There are two options for gluing glass to the surface:

1. Spreading the glue on the surface and sticking the glass onto it

2. Spreading the glue onto the back of the glass and placing it on the surface.

When using the first, quicker method, it would be wise to spread the glue on relatively small areas to keep it from drying prematurely.

The second method is slower, buy allows for precision in the size of the pieces before placing them.

Both methods are viable, and everyone is free to choose which suits them best. If you require an accurate placement, you should first adjust it and then spread it with glue. If you need to fill a large area with random or identical shapes (e.g. squares), feel free to spread on the surface and place the pieces.

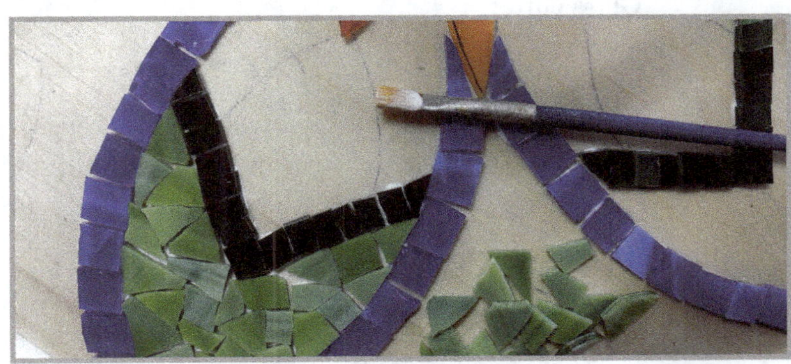

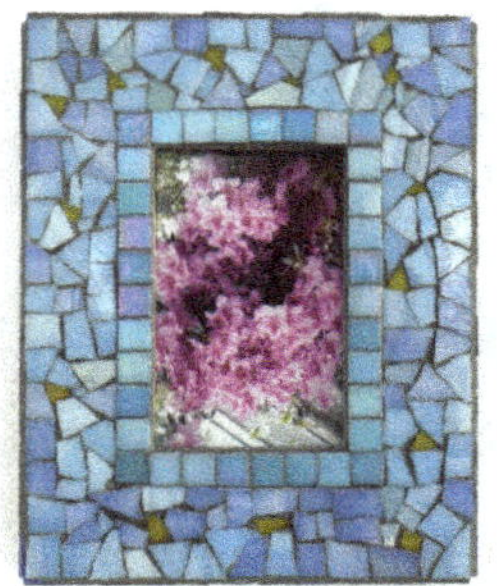

Project No. 5: Blue Picture Frame

Trying to come up with a gift for your grandparents? Maybe something to put around that picture of your loved ones on your desk? I bet you'd enjoy making a picture frame for a photo you like. This is a relatively simple piece. We mix readymade glass tiles with cut glass, and learn to cut glass with a knife for coating the side of the frame. To make the photo in the frame stand out, I chose a low-key design in light azure with dark blue on the sides and a touch of yellow.

Materials:

A wooden picture frame, external width of 25.5 x 20.5 cm / 8" x 10"

Glass in shades of blue, two shades of azure, a bit of yellow glass

Azure glass tiles, measurements 1.5 x 1.5 cm / 0.6" x 0.6"

Strong white glue

Brush

Nipper

Glass cutter

T-square

Running pliers

Gray Grout

Grout Equipment: Mixing bowl, water, a wooden stick, rags, gloves

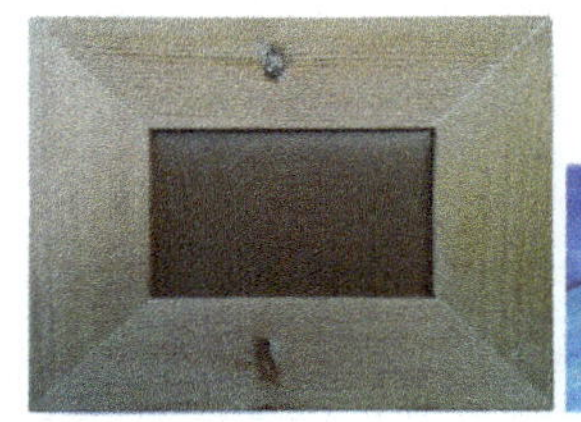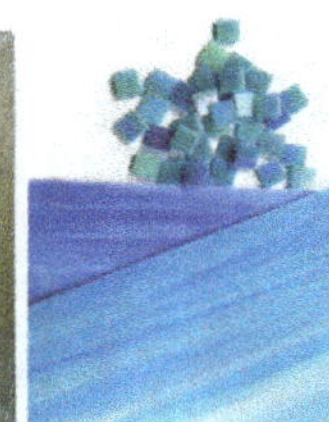

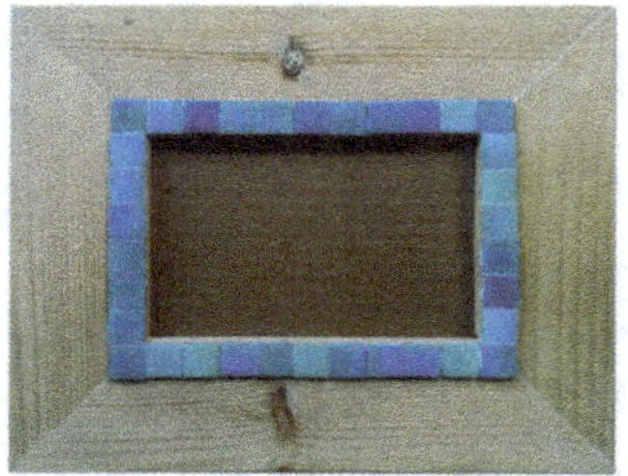

1 Before you begin, if there's a glass panel in the frame, remove and set it aside so not to soil it during the work. Glue the azure tiles around the inner frame with white glue.

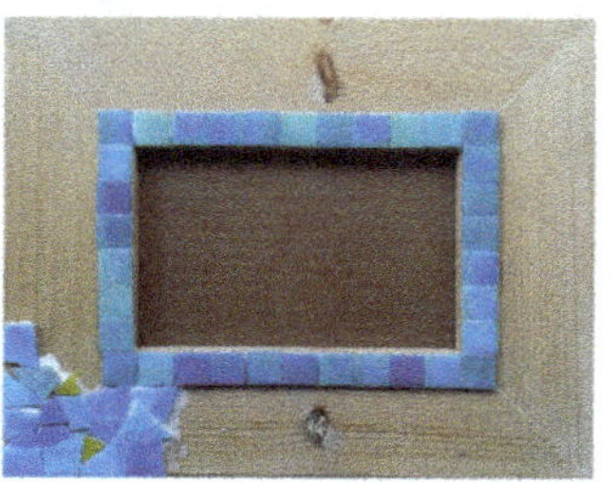

2 Cut the two shades of azure glass into random little pieces. Opt for blended, non-smooth glass rather than uniform tiles, in order to get a more vivid, colorful look. Cut those into tiny pieces, as well as a few pieces of yellow glass.

3 Glue the azure glass onto the frame; mix shades. Make sure to keep a straight line in the outer frame. You can spread glue on a small area and stick the glass to it, then repeat in next area. Occasionally add a small yellow glass piece.

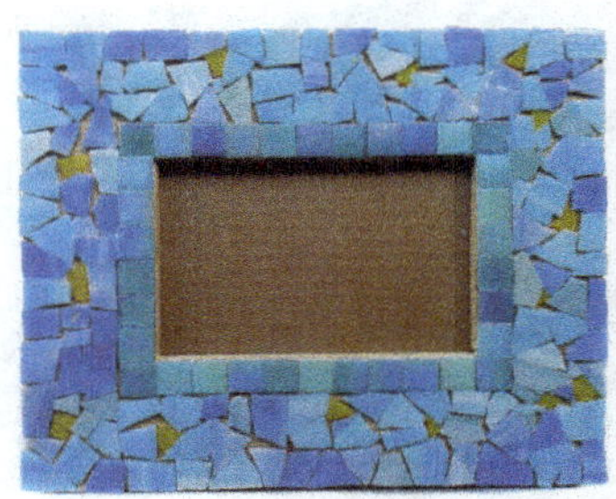

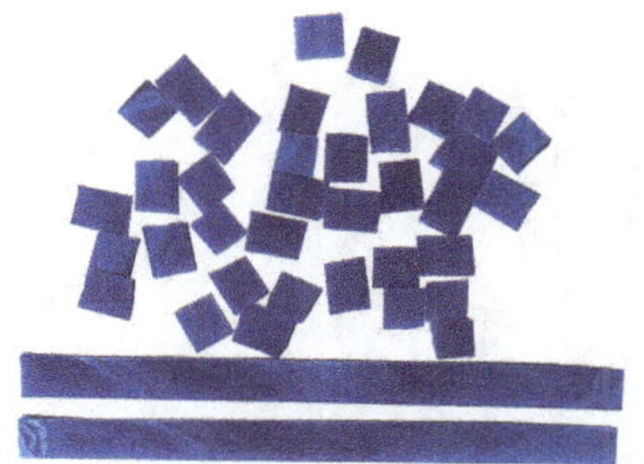

4 Once you're done with gluing the frame, start preparing the glass bits for gluing the sides. For this purpose, use the glass cutter to cut strips of blue glass as thick as the frame (see instructions on cutting glass with glass cutter on page 33). Then cut the strips into rectangles of varying lengths.

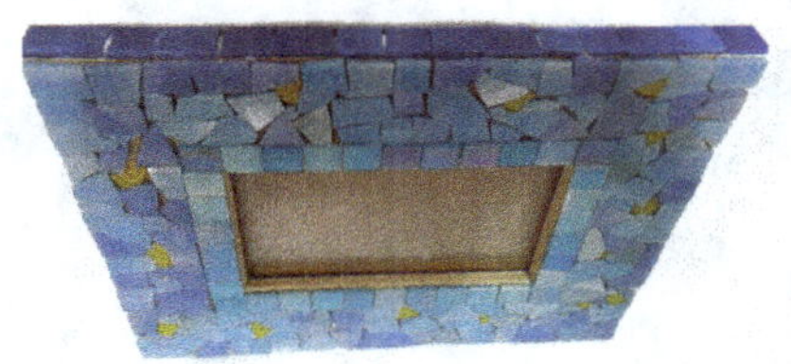

5 Glue the blue rectangles on the frame edges, maintaining a straight line. Leave to dry for 24 hours.

6 Prepare gray grout according to manufacturer instructions. It's essential that you smooth out the bevel created between the azure glass in the front and the blue glass surrounding the frame. When done, clean thoroughly and polish with a wet rag.

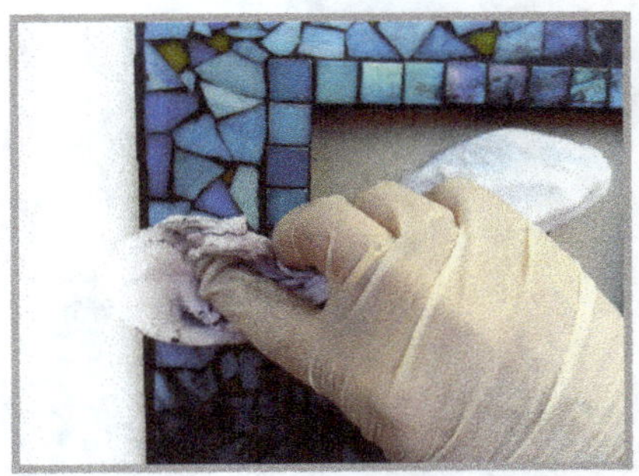

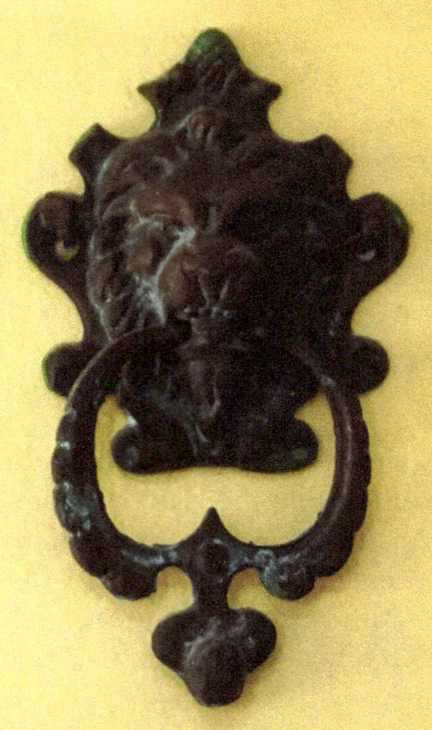

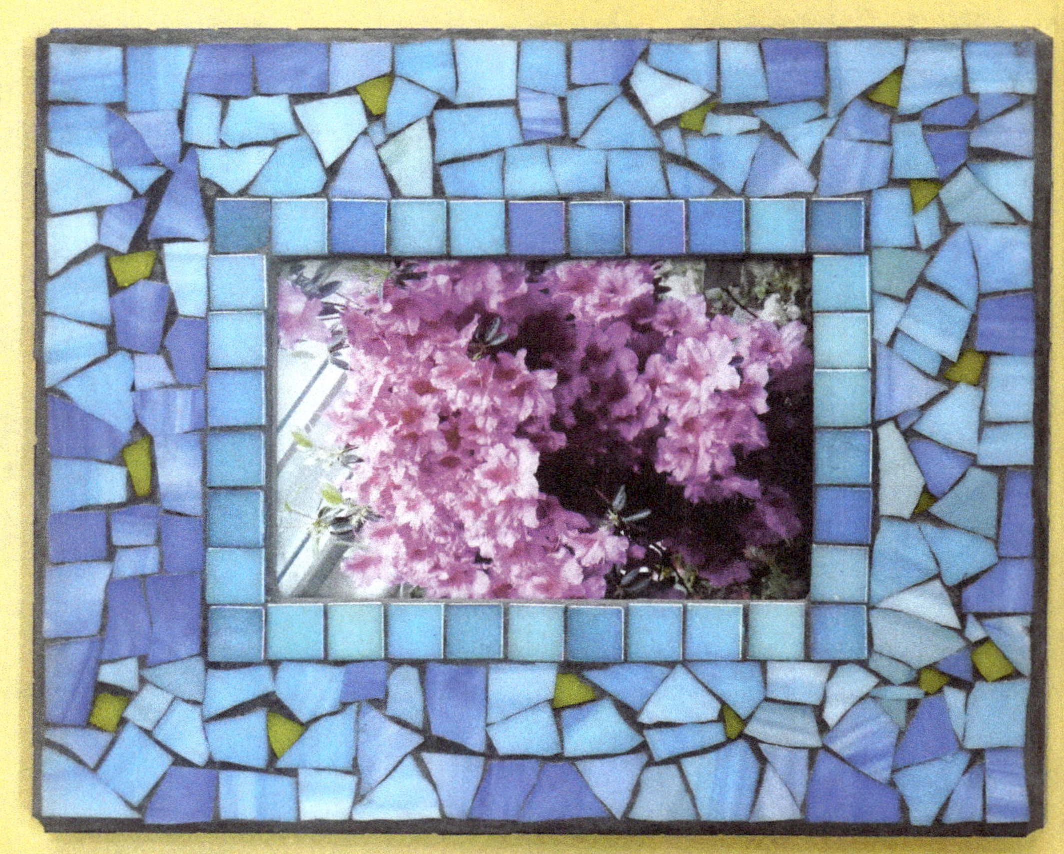

Cutting Glass with Glass Cutter

Unlike with ceramics, glass is cut by using the glass cutter to make a groove and snapping apart the two pieces it divides.

Glass cutting methods are a staple of stained glass and mosaic crafting. To achieve optimal accuracy, an electric sander is used. This book does not cover that, but sticks to cutting the glass with the cutter and nipper alone.

There are various types of glass cutters and grips. A high-end cutter is recommended for making the process more convenient.

Glass Cutting Stages – Straight Line:

TIP: It's a good idea to practice first on plain, clear glass.

1. Place the glass you want to cut on a clean, level surface.

2. In order to cut a straight, accurate line, use a framing square or T-square: Place the square on the glass where you wish to cut. 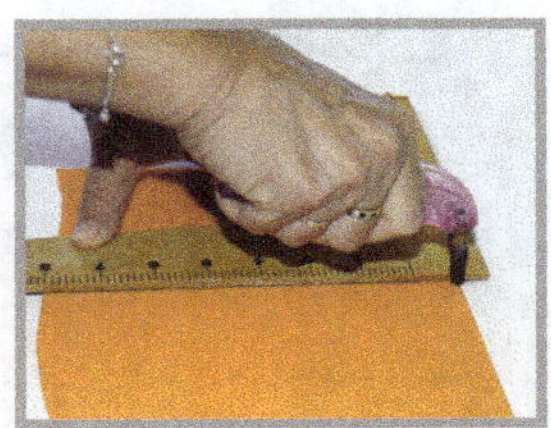

3. Hold the glass cutter with your dominant hand and dip it in oil if necessary (required with certain types of cutters).

4. Place the cutter at the top or bottom edge of the glass and hold it straight, perpendicular to the glass.

5. Groove the glass lengthwise with your dominant hand, while pressing on the square with your other hand to keep it in place. You can cut either from top to bottom or vice-versa. It's essential to do this while maintaining even pressure from edge to edge, otherwise the cut might become crooked. If you hear a slight ripping sound, you're doing it right. 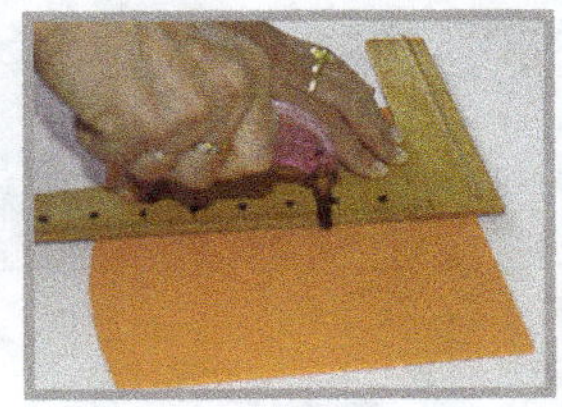

6. Grab the glass by its bottom with running pliers and snap it off. Note that the markings in the pliers are facing upward. The glass will snap in two along the line.

Cutting Glass Strips by Size:

1. Place the glass you wish to cut on a clean, level surface. 

2. Using a glass marker and T-square, mark the width you want to cut. You can mark all the desired lines in advance.

3. Place the T-square on the glass. Begin cutting the strips in order as explained before. Leave the wide part of the glass for last. Repeat stages 3-6 of glass cutting. 

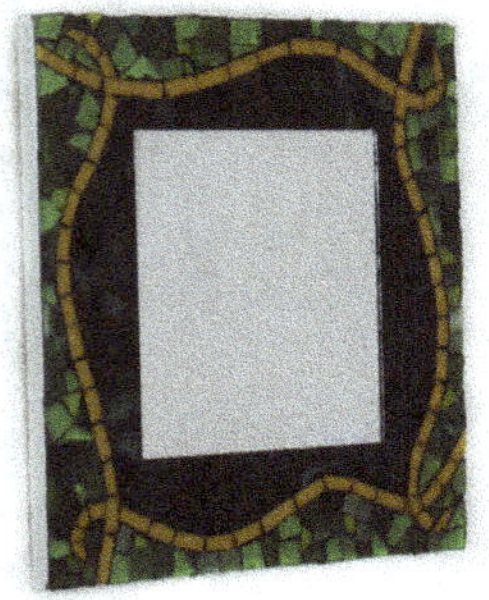

Project No. 6: Square Mirror

This mirror can be crafted to any size desirable. It's comprised of a square wooden board onto which the mirror is glued. You can place it beside your front door or as a wall ornament, and naturally you can change the color blends to whatever you choose. This work involves accurate cutting – for the yellow strips – and random cuts for everything else. Since the strips are very thin, heed the note below in order to cut uniform size strips.

** In the first photos, the mirror was covered just for the sake of shooting the photo – there's no need for you to do that.

Materials:

A wooden board, external measurements of 25.5 x 25.5 cm / 10" x 10"

A mirror measuring 15 x 15 cm / 6" x 6"

Glass in shades of yellow, dark green, several shades of light green

Strong white glue

Brush

Nipper

Glass cutter

T-square

Running pliers

Black Grout

Grout Equipment: Mixing bowl, water, a wooden stick, rags, gloves

Pattern for the mirror:
Enlarge on a photocopier by 350% for a full size design

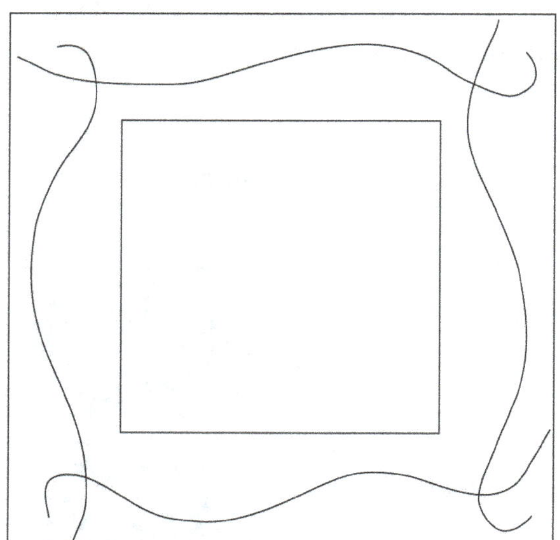

1 Copy the pattern to the wooden board using tracing paper. Glue the mirror at the center.

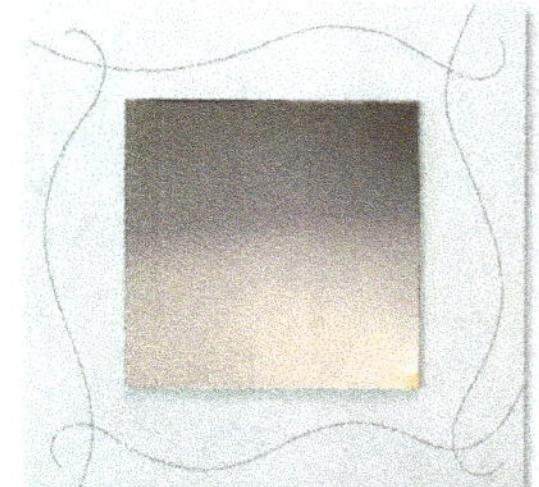

2 Cut the yellow glass into thin strips, about 7 mm / 0.27" thick (instructions on page 37).

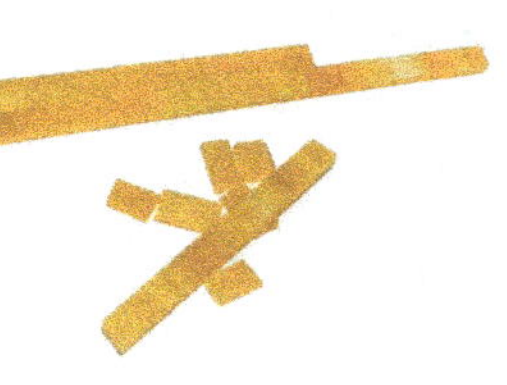

3 Cut the strips into rectangles using the nipper – no need to maintain uniform length.

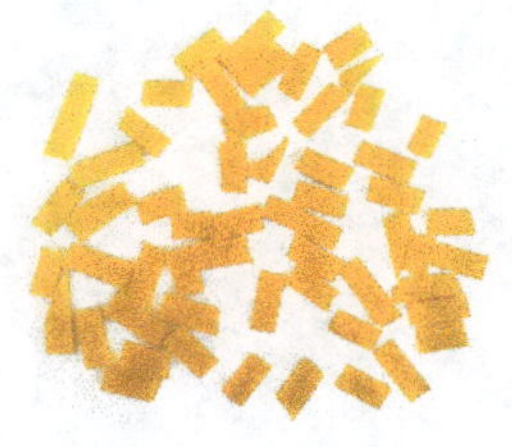

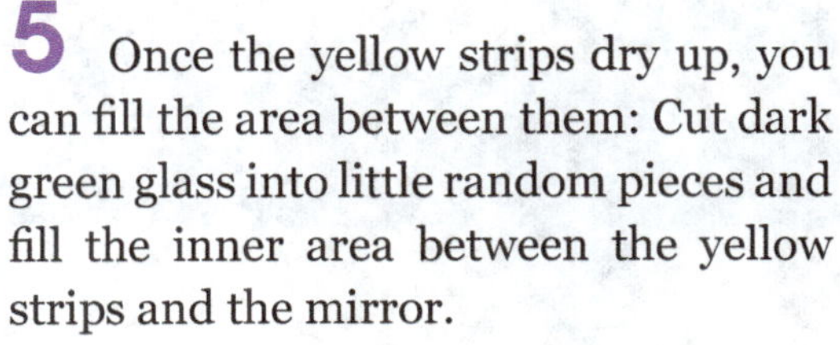

4 Glue the yellow glass strips along the lines. At the end of each line, glue a pointy piece.

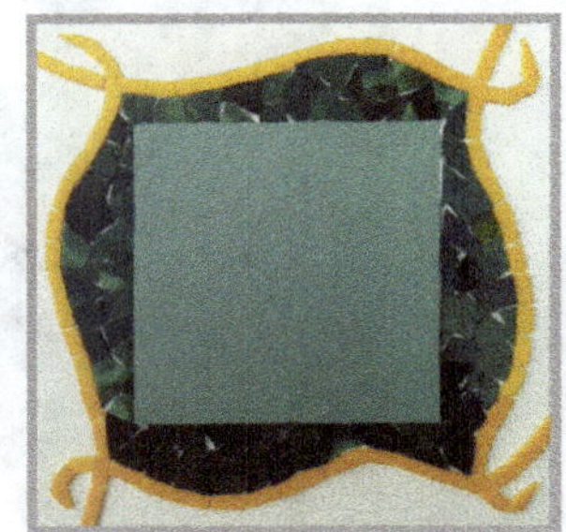

5 Once the yellow strips dry up, you can fill the area between them: Cut dark green glass into little random pieces and fill the inner area between the yellow strips and the mirror.

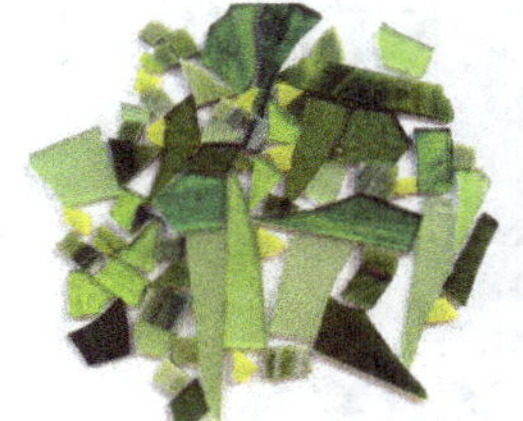

6 Cut green glass in various shades into little pieces. You can use leftover glass if you have some.

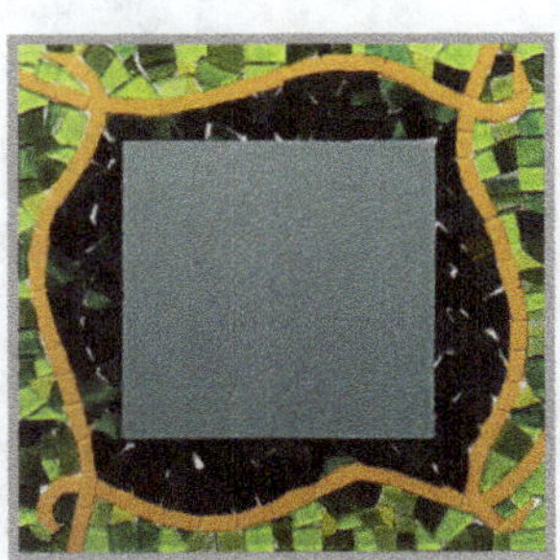

7 Glue the green glass in the remaining area. Leave to dry for 24 hours.

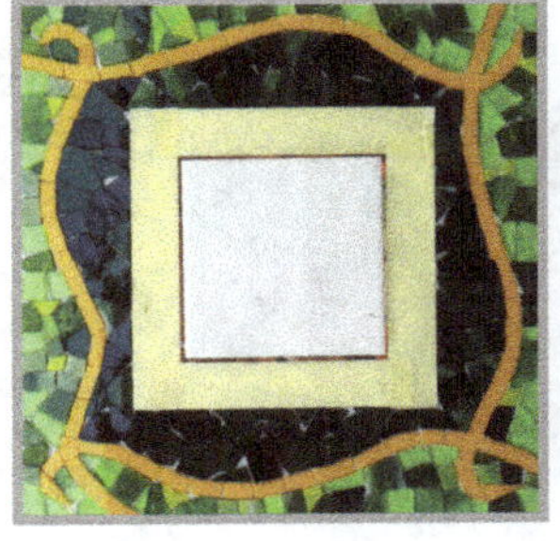

8 Before preparing the grout, cover the edges of the mirror to avoid soiling it: Stick some masking tape on it and glue an accurate frame on the mirror's edges.

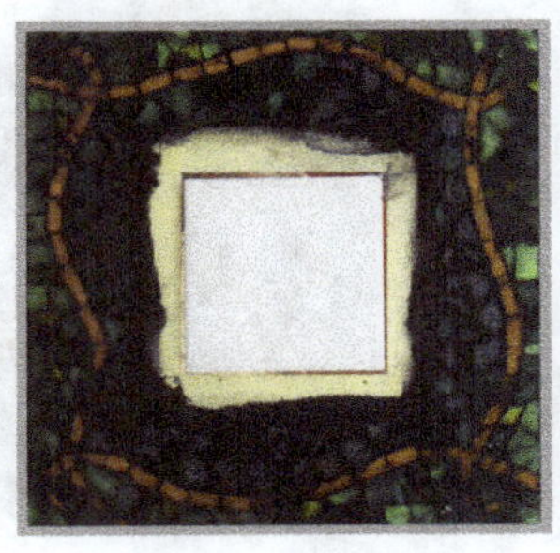

9 Prepare black grout according to manufacturer instructions and carefully spread over the frame.

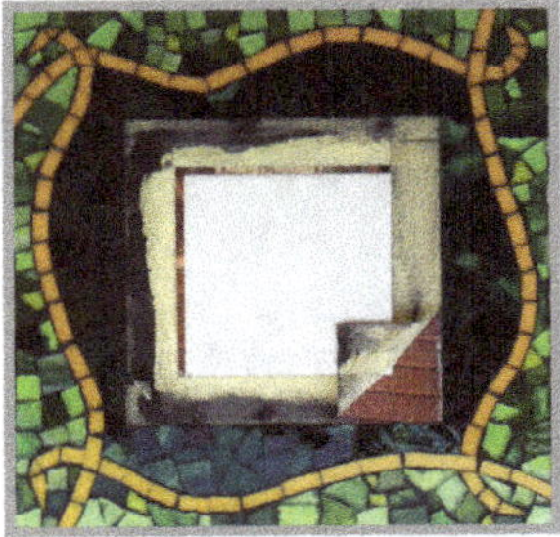

10 When done, peel the masking tape and attach a hanger to the back.

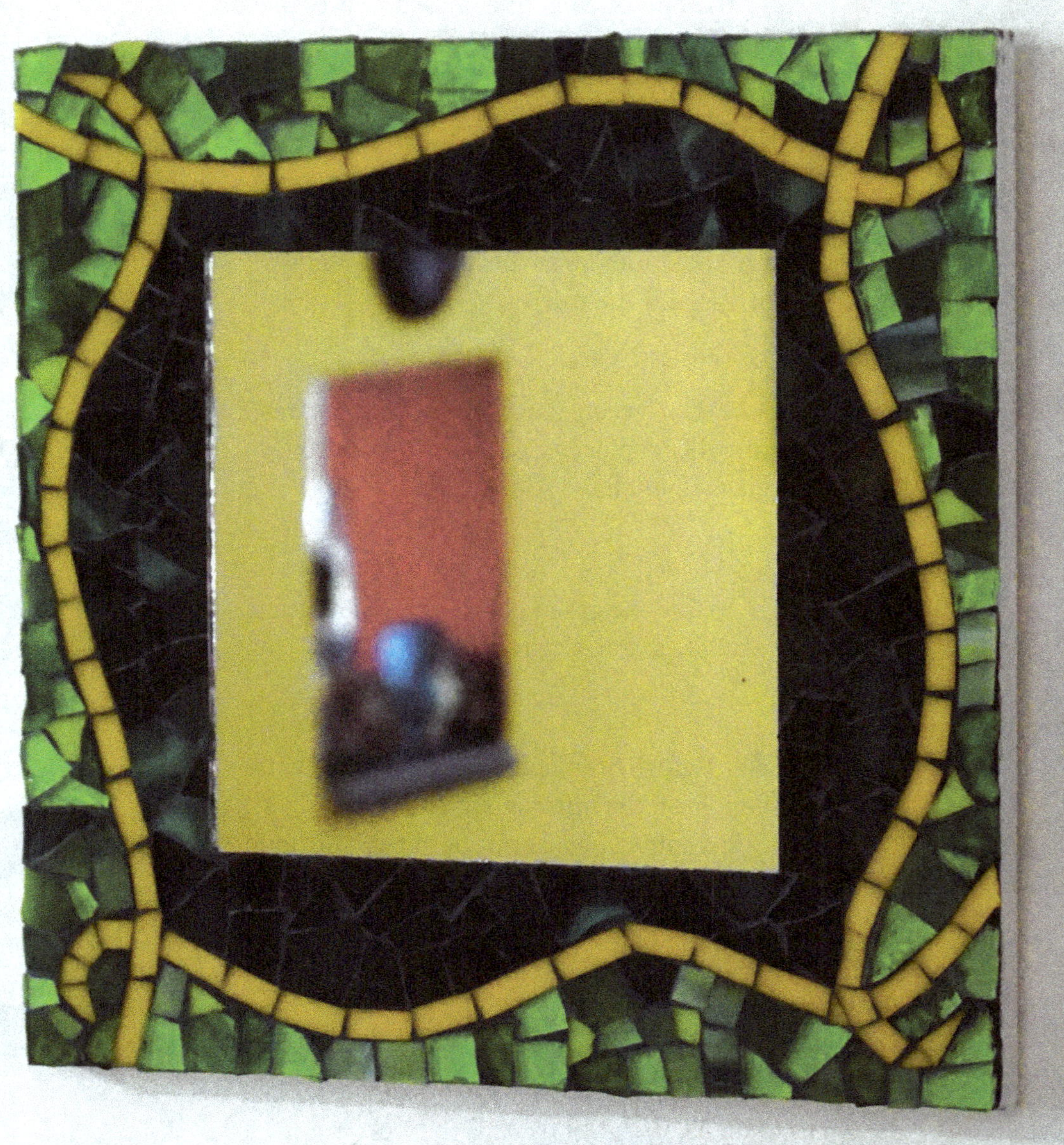

Cutting Glass into Thin Strips

You can cut thin strips using the conventional method using T-square. Since you're slicing thin, and it's sometimes hard to see the exact spot when it comes down to millimeters, I suggest using a small square object in the desired width and using that as a ruler.

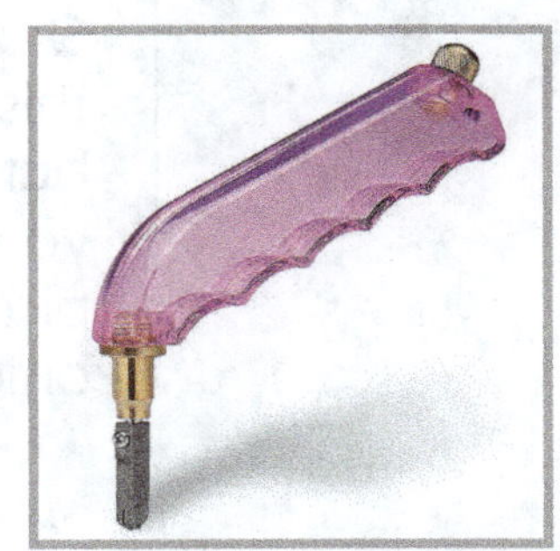

Take into account that the strip you cut will be narrower than the square object, since the blade of the glass cutter is at the center of the instrument, a few millimeters away from the T-square.

1. Align the square to the top side of the glass. Place the square object adjacent to the square, so that it just reaches the edge of the glass.

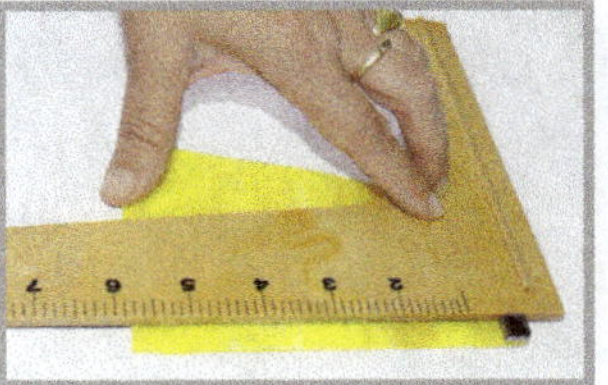

2. Remove the square object, groove the glass with the cutter and snap the strip.

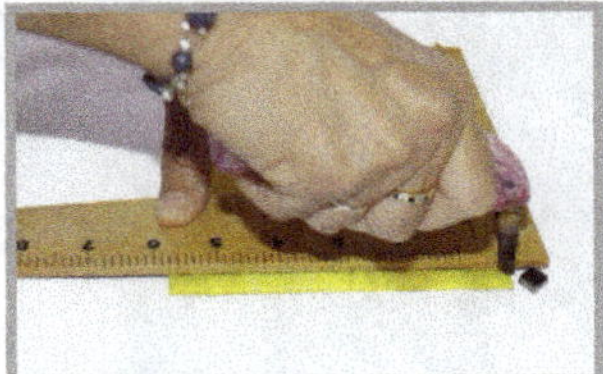

3. Repeat this action for every individual cut. If you maintain accuracy, the strips will be uniform in size and you won't need to mark out lines at all.

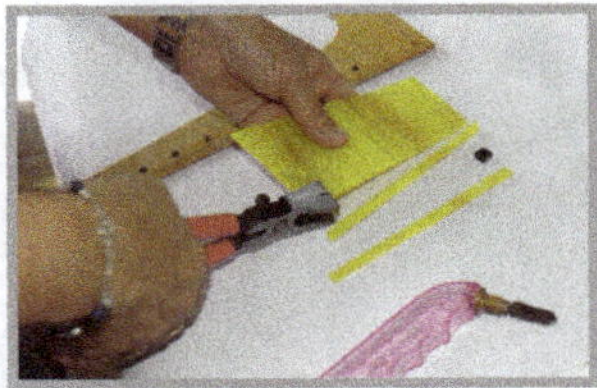

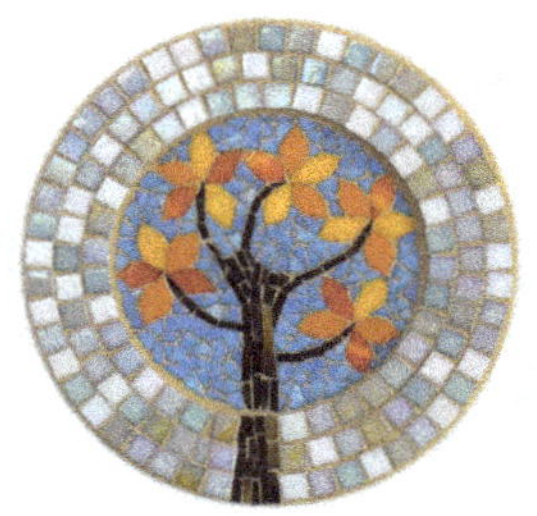

Project No. 7: Round Picture

This picture will require use of several materials and techniques: Glass tiles, precisely cut glass and randomly cut glass pieces. This combination makes for an interesting picture – not too large, but very present. I went with fall-colored leaves, but obviously you can choose whatever colors you desire. I chose a wooden plate with a wide edge, but you can just as well glue the work onto a round wooden plate.

Materials:

A round wooden board measuring 27 cm / 10.5" in diameter

Glass tiles measuring 1.4 cm / 0.55" in shades of white, light yellow and light green

Glass in shades of azure, brown, several shades of orange

Strong white glue

Tracing paper

Glass marker

Pencil

Brush

Nipper

Glass cutter

Running pliers

Breaker-Grozier Pliers

Light brown grout

Grout Equipment: Mixing bowl, water, a wooden stick, rags, gloves

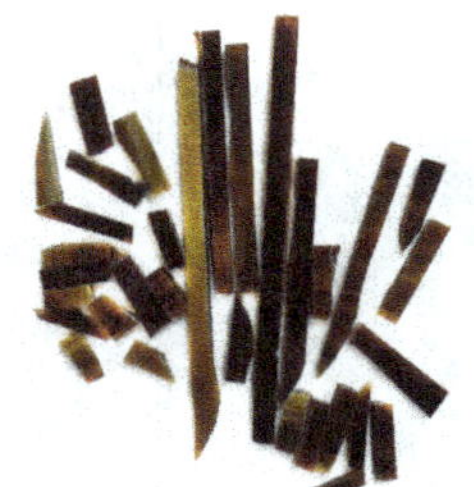

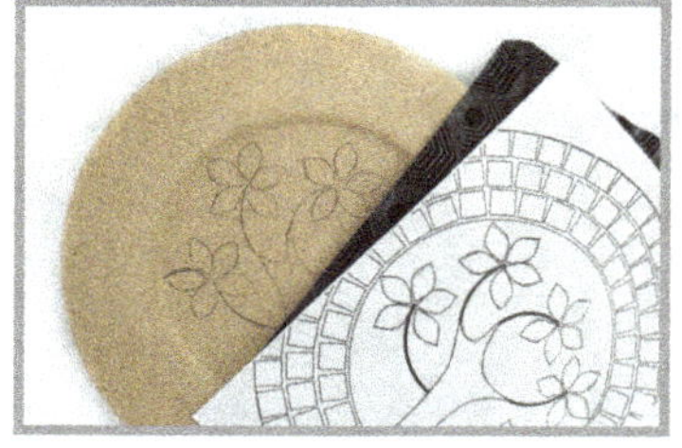

1 Print and copy the pattern to the round board using tracing paper and a pencil.

2 Tree: Cut long strips of brown glass using the glass cutter, then small rectangles using the wheeled glass nipper.

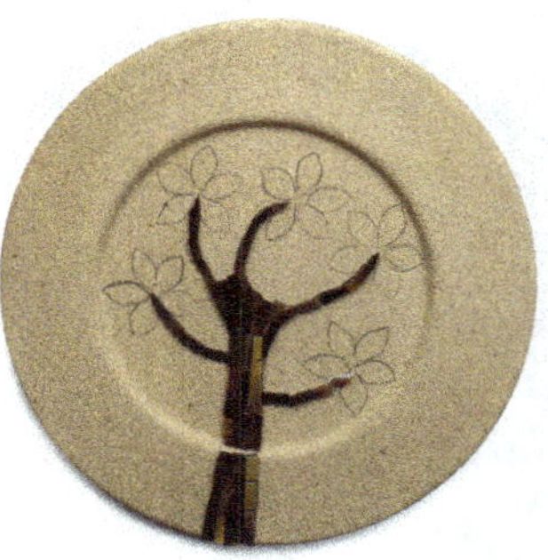

3 Paste the strips to the tree trunk lengthwise. Opt for glass with various shades of brown. Finish every branch with a pointy piece of glass.

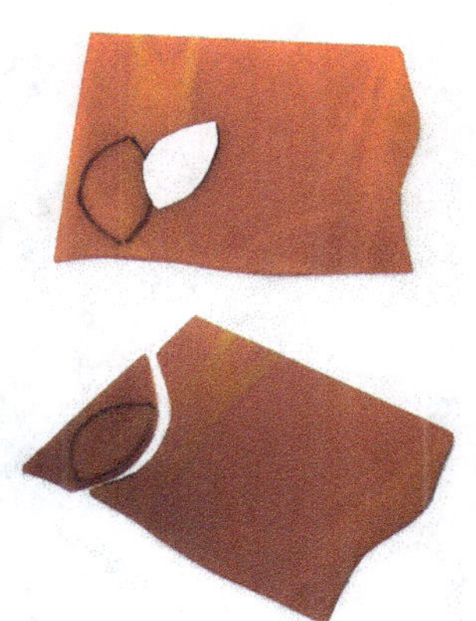

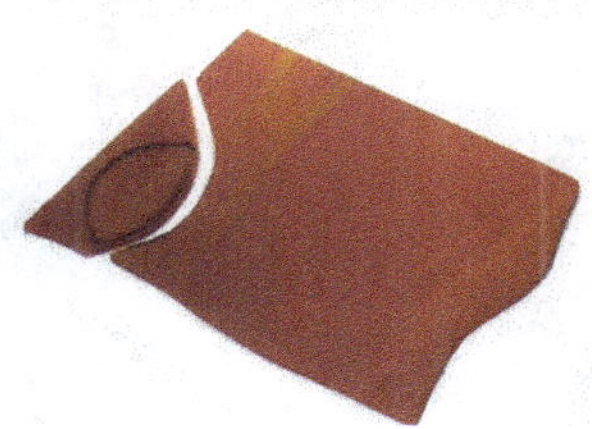

4 Leaves: These will be cut accurately, each leaf individually. Cut a paper leaf from the printed pattern and mark its shape on the orange glass with a marker.

5 Make the first cut bottom-to-top, along the right curve of the leaf. Separate the two parts of the glass with a breaker-grozier (see instructions for cutting glass below).

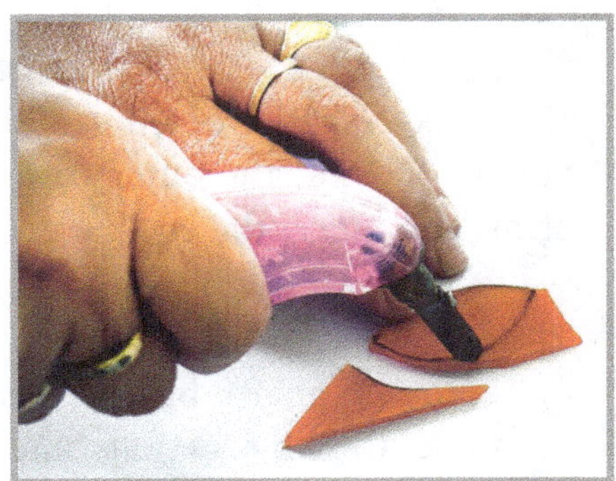

6 Complete the leaf shape with one or two cuts, depending on the location of the leaf on the glass (if it's near an edge, opt for two cuts).

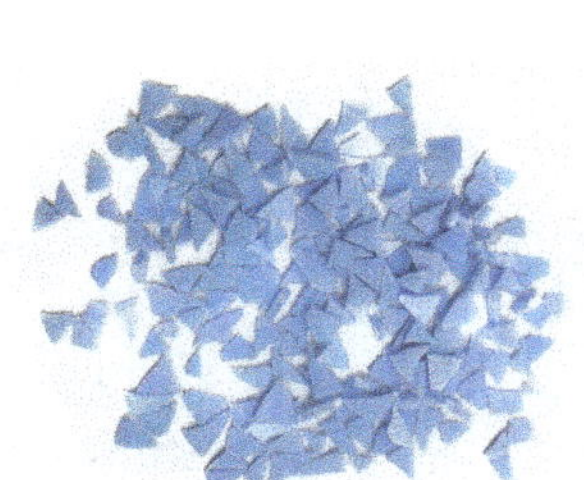

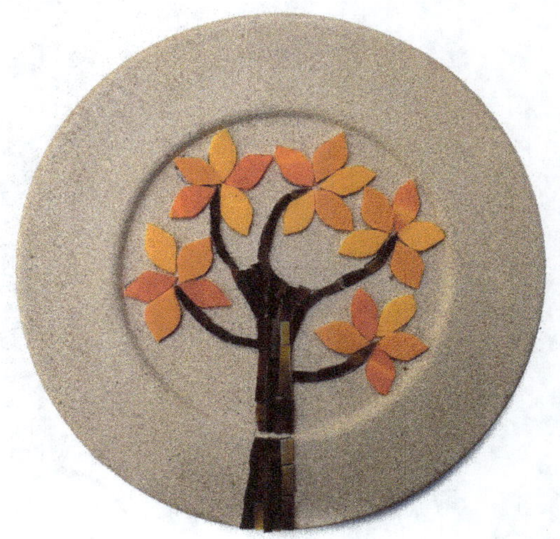

8 Background: Cut azure glass into small, random shapes, mainly triangles.

7 Cut leaves in different shades and paste onto the wood according to the example.

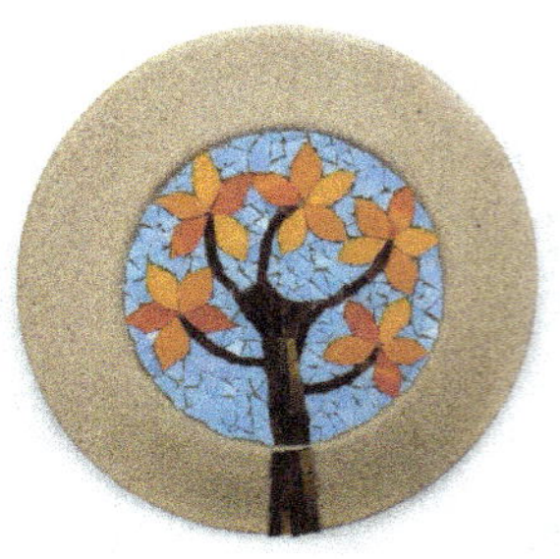

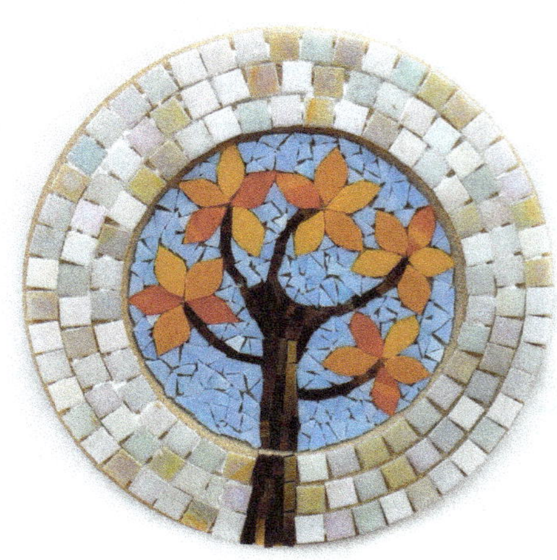

9 Paste around the trunk and leaves.

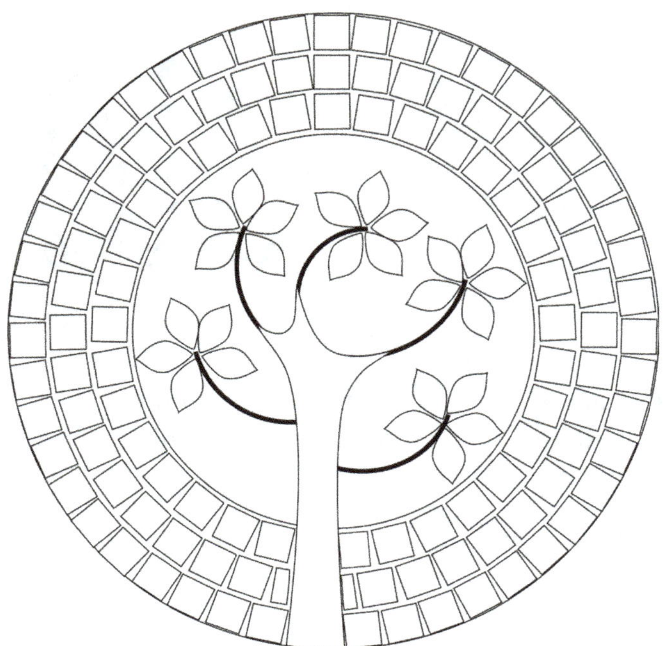

10 Frame: Paste three rows of glass tiles with mixed shades of white, light green and light yellow. Start at the outer row to keep the work straight to the end. Leave to dry for 24 hours.

11 Prepare brown grout according to manufacturer instructions and spread over the surface. Use a scraper to spread the grout to the edges as well, and create an appealing finish. Clean thoroughly with a wet rag.

Pattern for the picture: Enlarge on a photocopier by 320% for a full size design

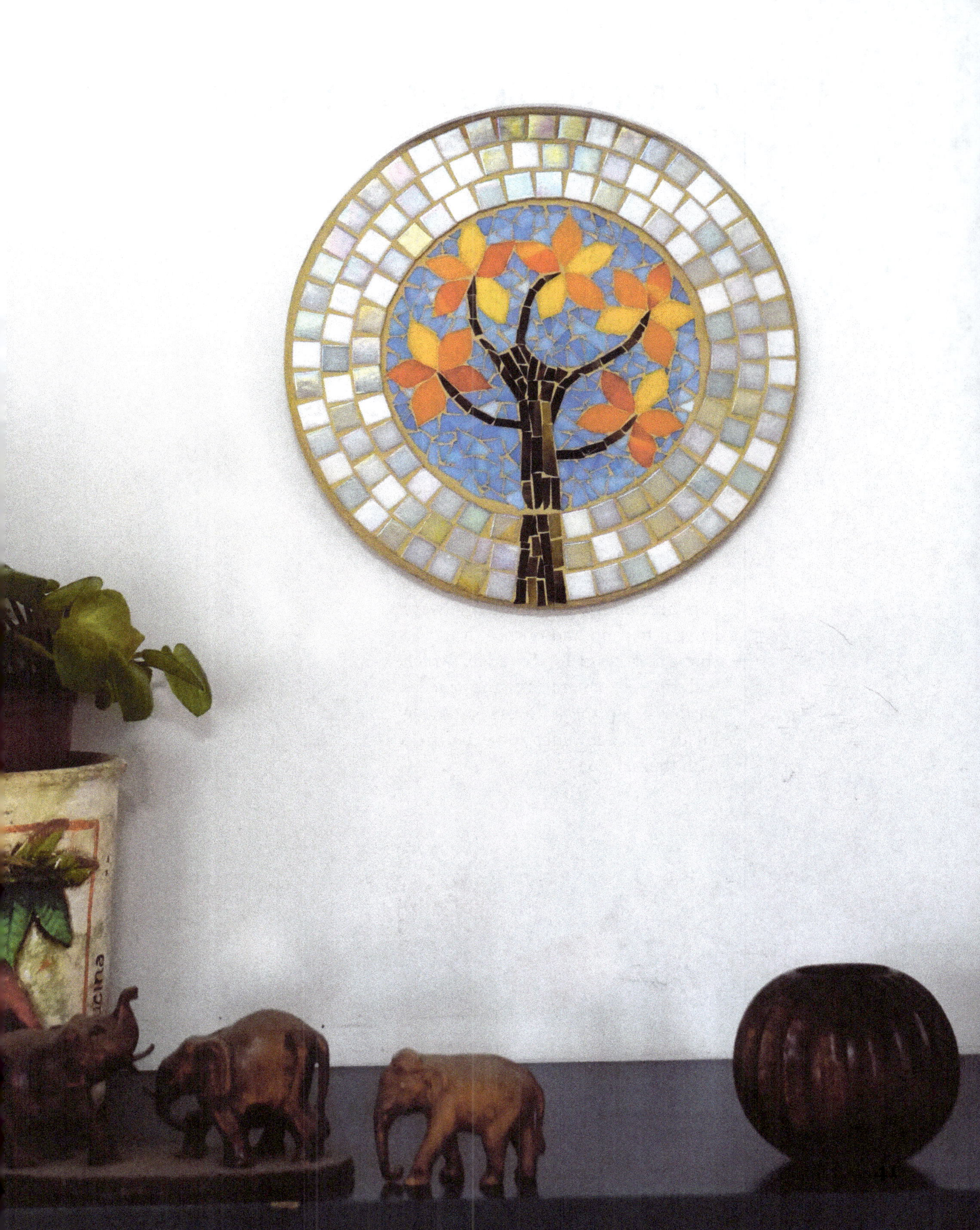

Cutting Glass into Shapes and Using the Pliers

When cutting glass, we don't cut the way we would in ceramics, for example, but rather groove it and use the glass cutter or pliers to separate the two parts.

Because of this, some shapes take several steps to cut and it's advised that you first practice on plain, clear glass.

The first step is to look at the desired shape and plan the cuts ahead so that the pieces come apart easily. If it's straight lines, we'll cut them one by one, and always from edge to edge. You can cut from top to bottom or vice-versa.

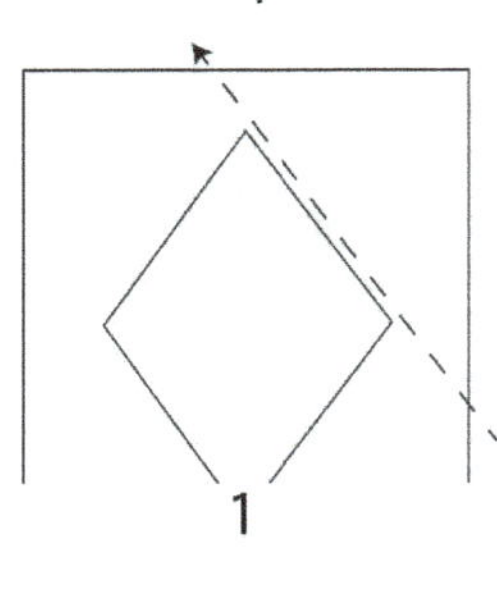

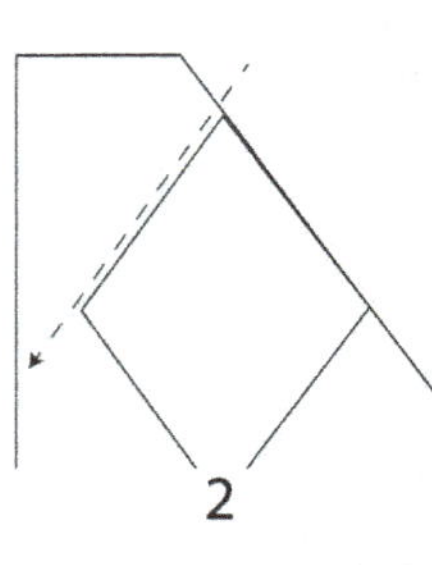

A round or curved shape is cut in a similar fashion – step by step. Always leave a margin and do not draw the shape too close to the edge, which will make separating the pieces harder. Keep the leftovers; later on, I'll give you a few ideas on what to do with them.

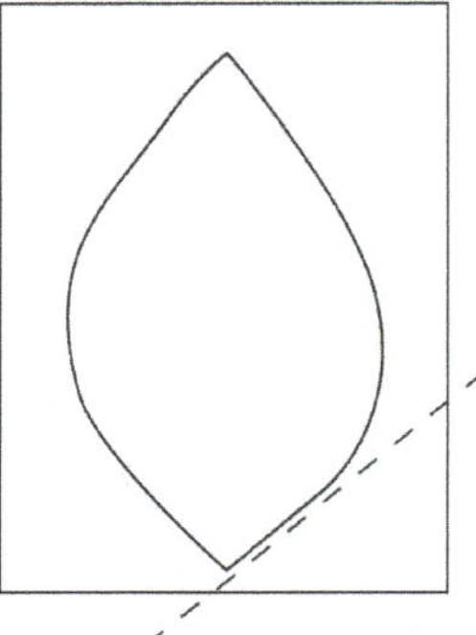

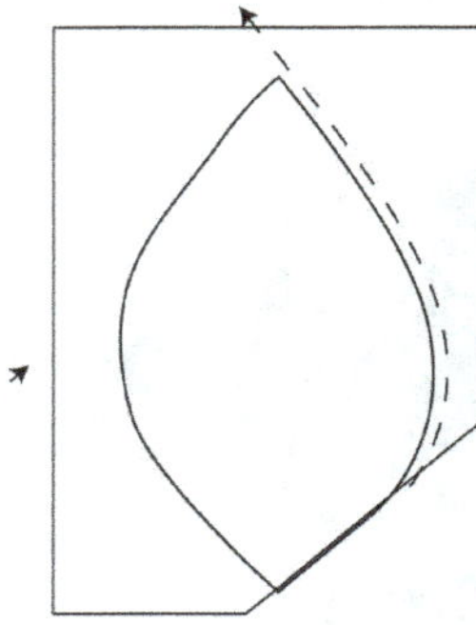

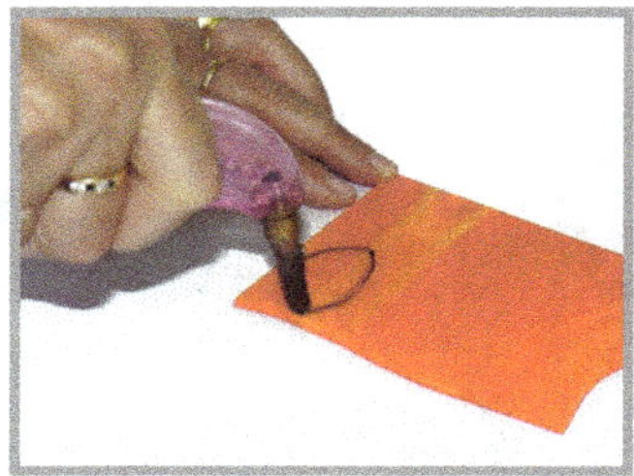
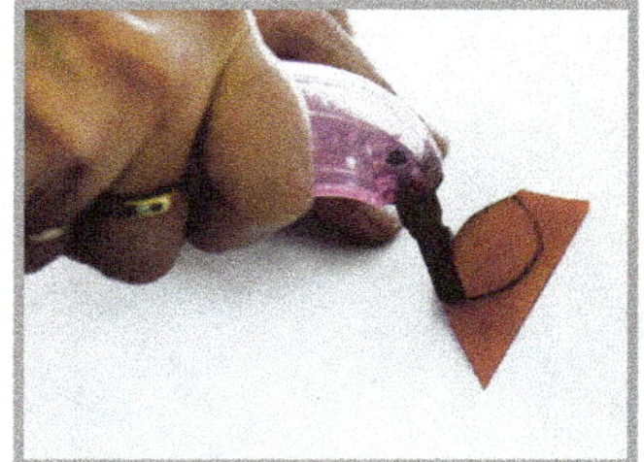
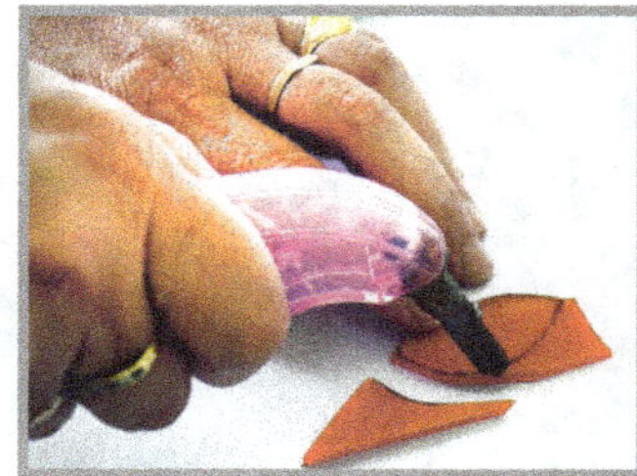

After performing the glass cutting, use the pliers to separate the pieces.

We work with two types of pliers:

1. **Running Pliers** – Used primarily to separate two straight, long pieces of glass. The top side is marked with a line, which should be aligned with the groove made with the glass cutter before applying pressure to separate the pieces. These pliers are made of either metal or plastic.

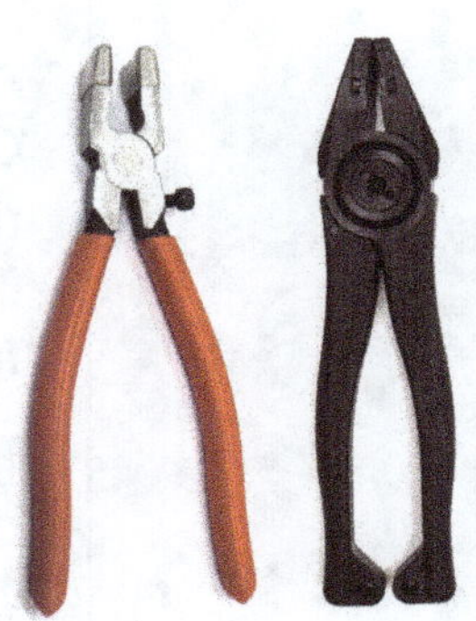

2. **Breaker-grozier pliers** – Very useful in working cutting glass into shapes. These pliers have two sides – one straight and one curved.

The straight side is meant to separate two pieces of glass, and the curved side is for chipping off small pieces from the shape to perfect it.

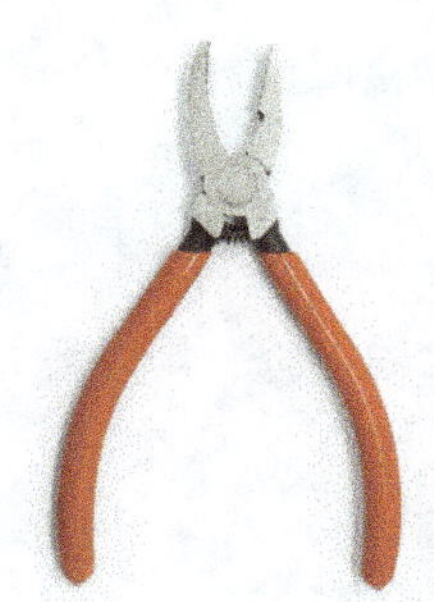

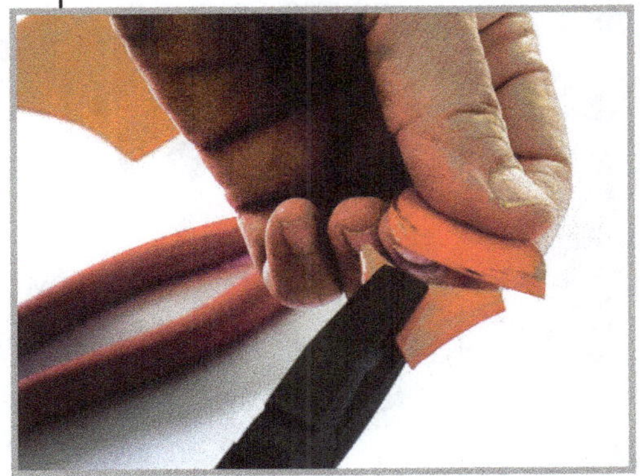

Work process: After grooving, hold the cut glass with one hand. Grab the pliers in the other hand, and pull downward. Most of the time, we'll use these pliers to separate the glass pieces, so make sure the straight side is pointing upward when cutting.

Project No. 8: Colorful Fishy Tray

A tray or a picture? That's up to you. This is a dual-purpose tray: On one hand it's practical, with a wooden base and a wide rim, so you can use it to serve coffee and cookies. On the other, it'll look pretty on a wall if you add a hanger – it already has a frame, right?

This piece may seem simple, but cutting the fish accurately can be challenging.

The black fish is accentuated by colorful glass strips. The fish strips are cut widthwise while the background is cut lengthwise, which makes the piece more interesting and attractive. Light brown grout adds a gentle touch to the entire picture. Naturally, you can craft this on a wooden board, frame and hang it.

Materials:

A wooden tray with an inner surface area of 27 x 10.5 cm / 10.6" x 4.2"

Black glass

Glass in various shades

Strong white glue

Brush

Red or white glass marker

Pencil

Tracing paper

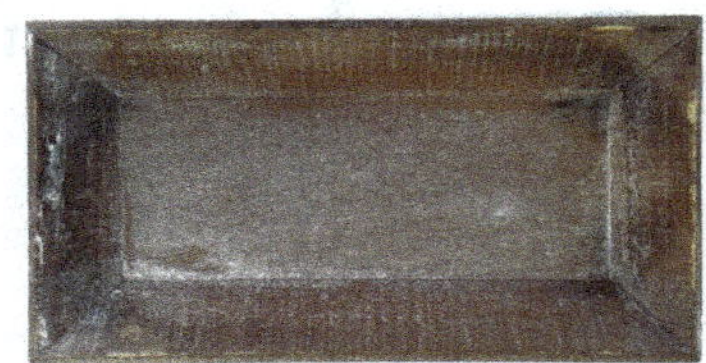

Nipper

T-square

Running pliers

Gray grout

Grout Equipment: Mixing bowl, water, a wooden stick, rags, gloves

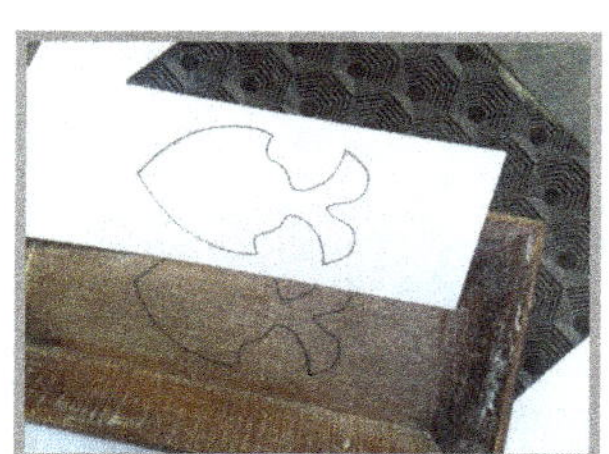

1 Copy the fish to the wooden tray with tracing paper.

2 Cut the paper fish and trace it on the black glass using the marker.

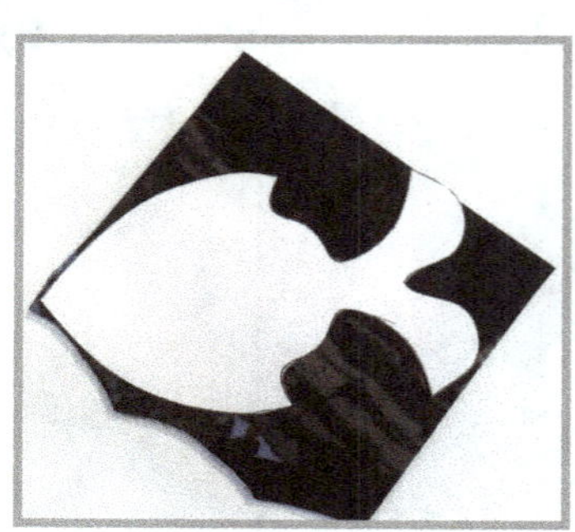

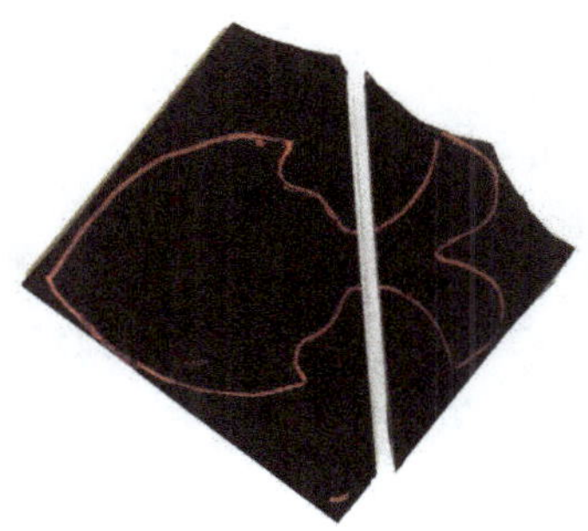

3 In order to cut the fish, first separate the body from the tail using a straight cut.

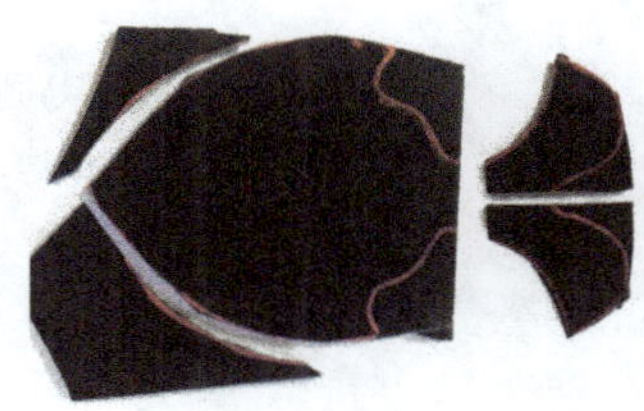

4 Now, begin cutting the fish body with short cuts along the edges using a glass cutter, little by little. Following each cut, break off the glass with a breaker-grozier

5 Finish the fish nice and clean. Cut the tail in two right down the middle.

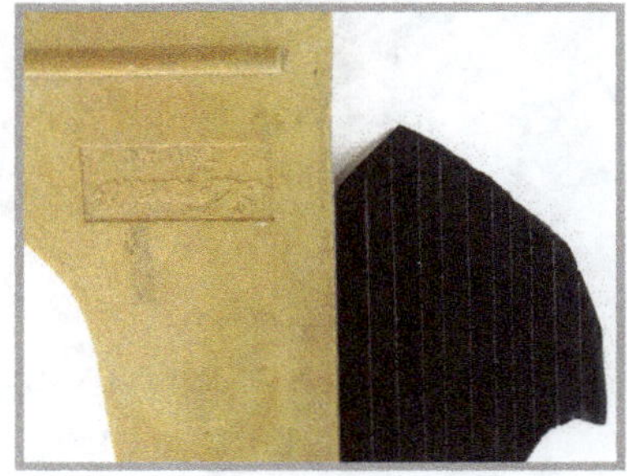

6 Cut the fish widthwise into even-height strips. You can create all the grooves first, then snap them one after the other. Leave the tail whole.

7 Using the nipper to cut every strip of black glass into small pieces and paste in place on the tray, according to the pattern. Glue both parts of the tail in place.

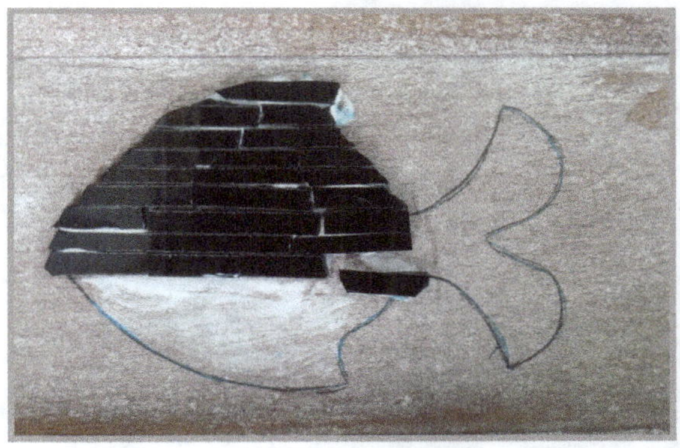

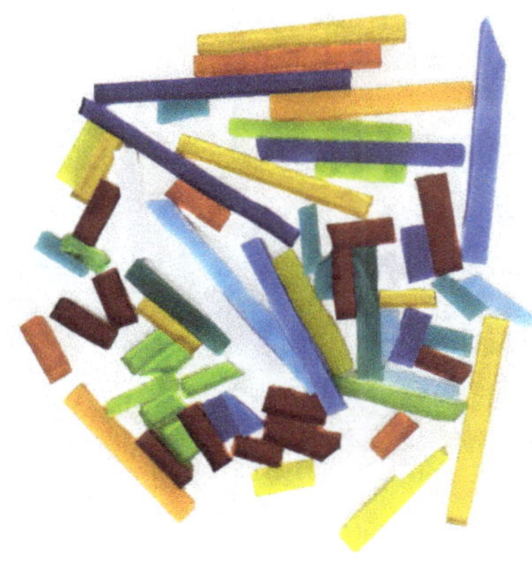

8 Background: Cut colorful glass in same-width stripes using the glass cutter. Then, cut those into smaller pieces using the nipper.

9 Paste the colored glass lengthwise on the tray. Make sure you match their size to the fish's contour by diagonally cutting with the nipper.

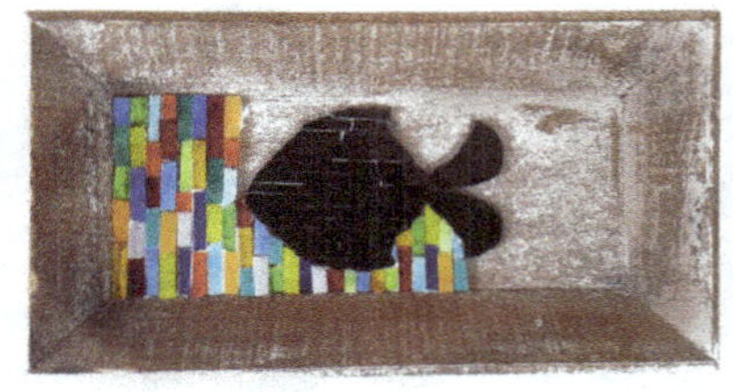

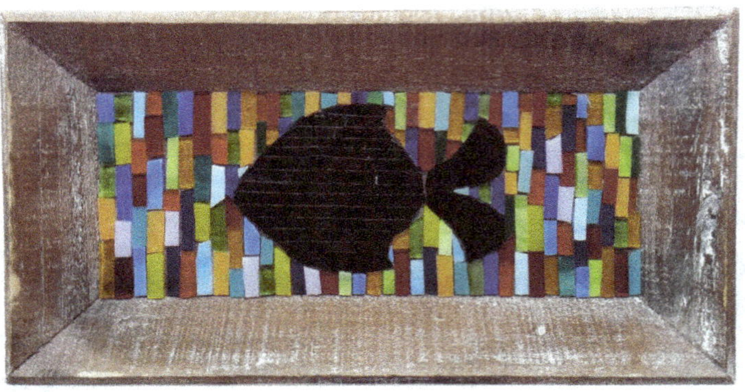

10 Finish gluing the background to the tray and leave to dry for 24 hours.

11 Prepare light brown grout according to manufacturer instructions, and spread over the tray.

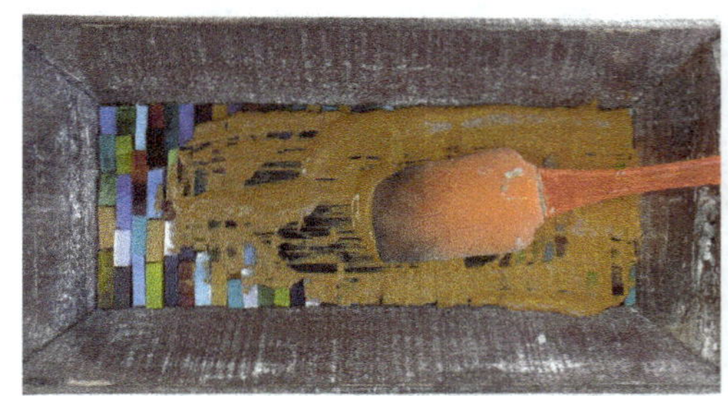

12 Clean thoroughly with a wet rag until the tray is nice and clean. If you intend to put it on a wall, now would be the time to attach a hanger in the back.

Pattern for the fish:
Enlarge on a photocopier by 165% for a full size design

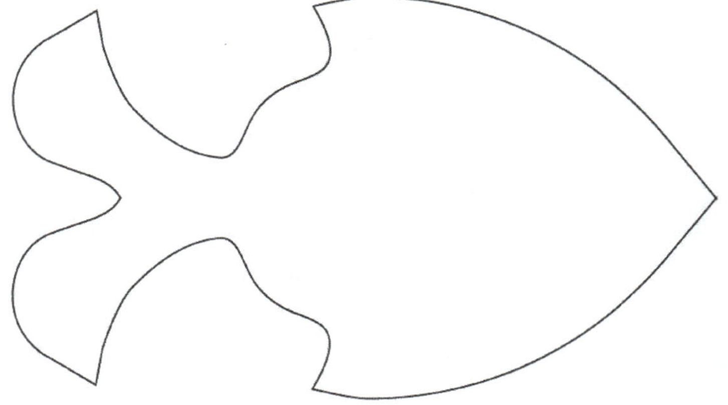

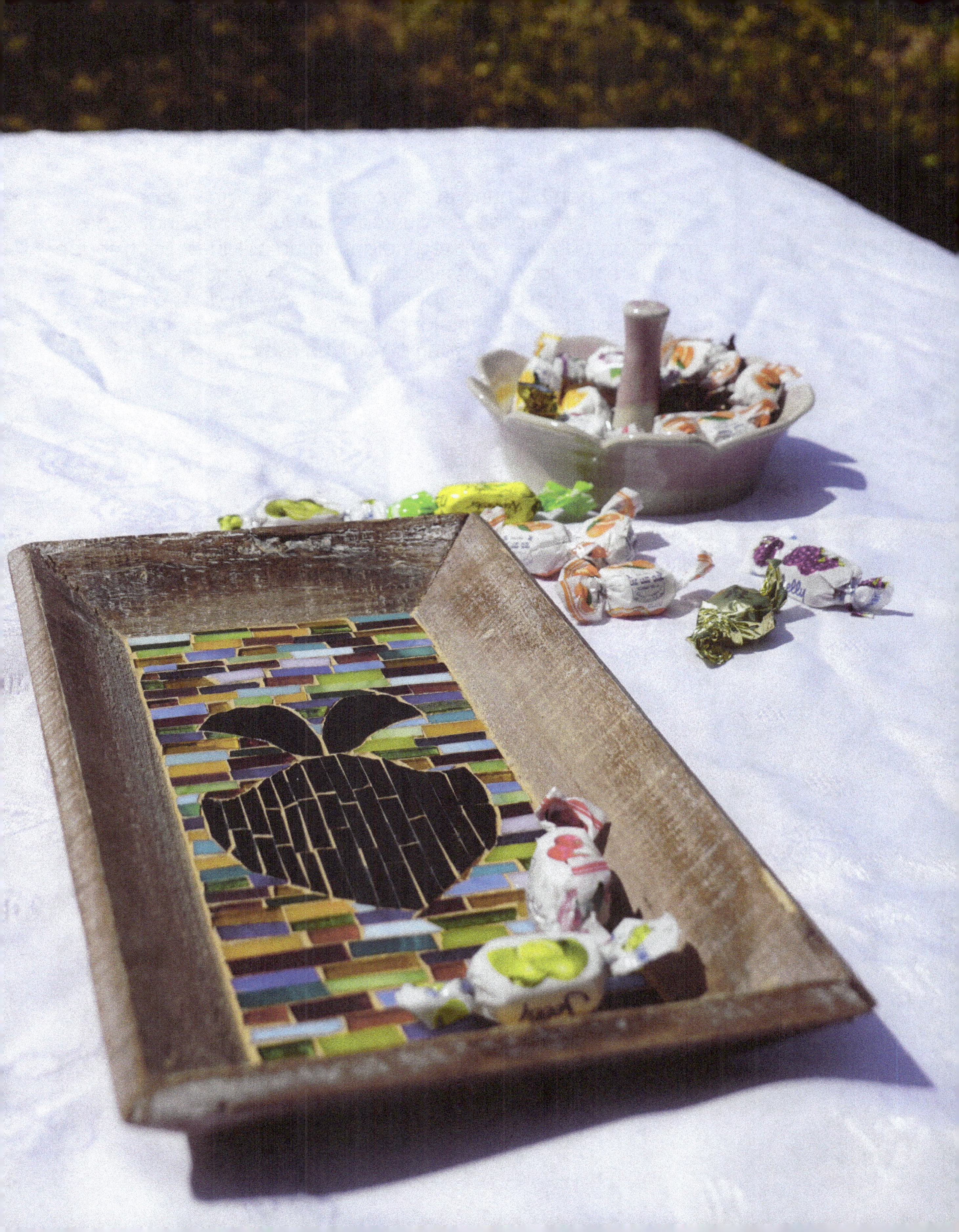

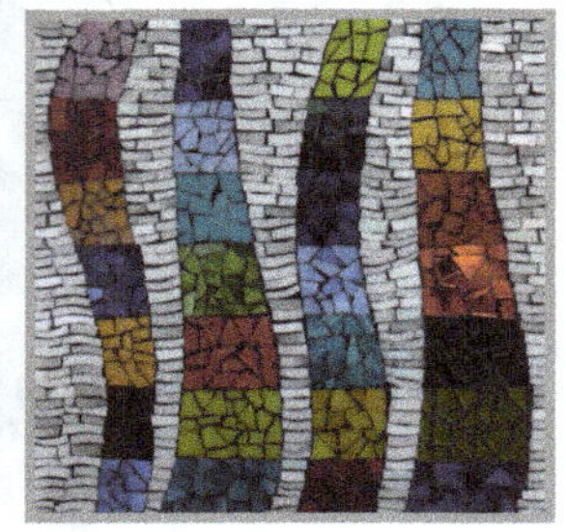

Project No. 9: Colorful Picture

This picture can be hung in any direction – lengthwise or widthwise. It's composed of curved, colorful longitudinal stripes, crossed and divided by fixed-height latitudinal lines. Each shape is a different color of glass. Its uniqueness, beyond being very colorful, is the use of two types of cuts: Random glass pieces for the colorful parts of the longitudinal lines, and widthwise strips for the white background. You can use any color and any combination you like.

Materials:

A wooden board measuring of 39 x 39 cm / 15.35" x 15.35"

Glass in various colors, white glass for the background (I used also white glass whose back side is a seashell texture)

Strong white glue

Brush

Pencil

Tracing paper

Nipper

Glass cutter

T-square

Running pliers

Black grout

Grout Equipment: Mixing bowl, water, a wooden stick, rags, gloves

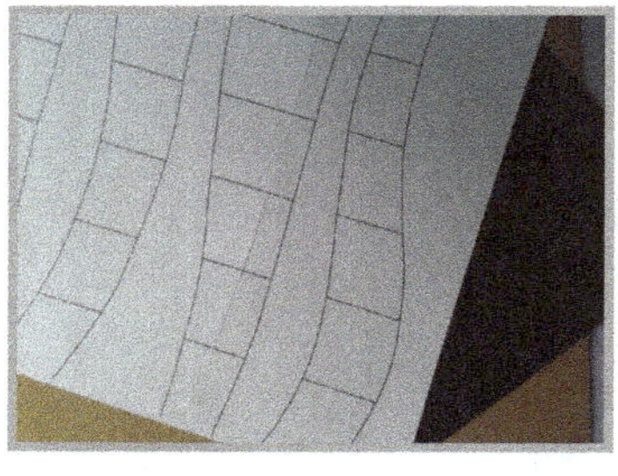

1 Print and copy to the wooden board using tracing paper.

2 Plan in advance the colors you want to make up the picture with, and cut each into small pieces.

TIP: Use a compartment box to keep the glass pieces. It's convenient and eliminates the need for a bunch of small boxes.

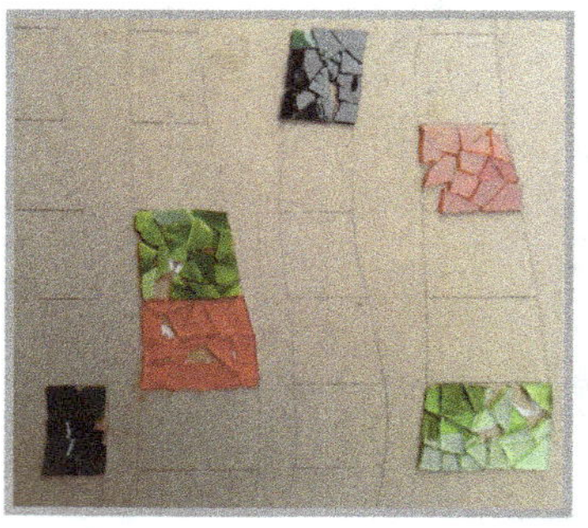

3 Begin gluing the colorful glass, each color in place. Make sure you keep the lines straight at the top and bottom of each area. You can repeat the same color several times.

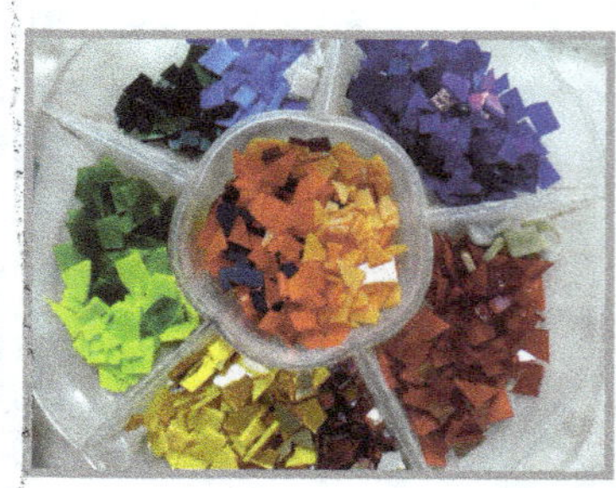

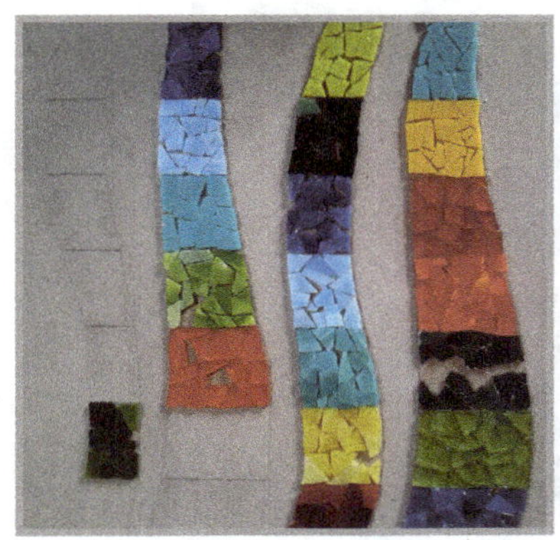

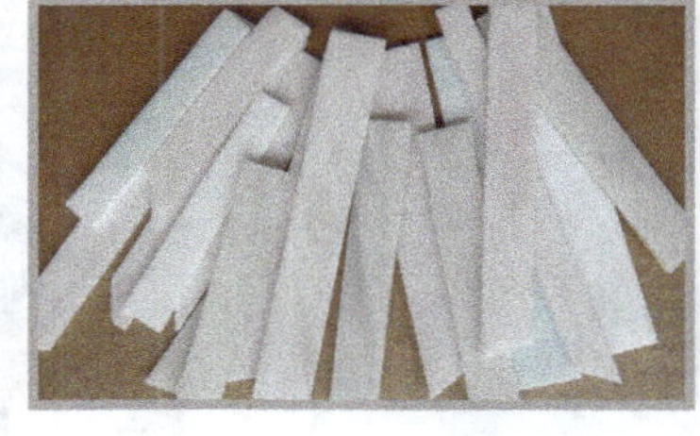

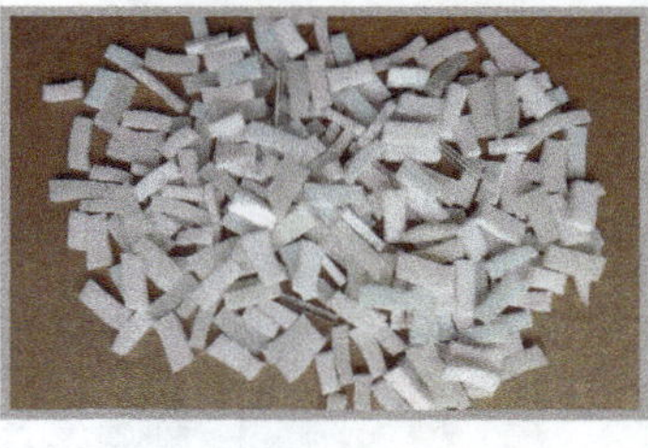

4 It's not necessary to glue the shapes by any order. Sometimes it's more convenient to glue several separate areas, so you don't push any pieces by accident. Finish gluing the colorful stripes.

5 Background: Using a square and glass cutter, cut white glass into strips. No need to maintain a uniform size; 1.-2.5 cm would do.

6 Cut the glass strips into little pieces using the nipper, all with the same orientation, several millimeters wide. Some pieces will turn out a bit rounded, and that's fine.

7 The white glass for the background should be glued widthwise. Cut the glass to the desired size to complete each row. Make sure you keep the frame straight.

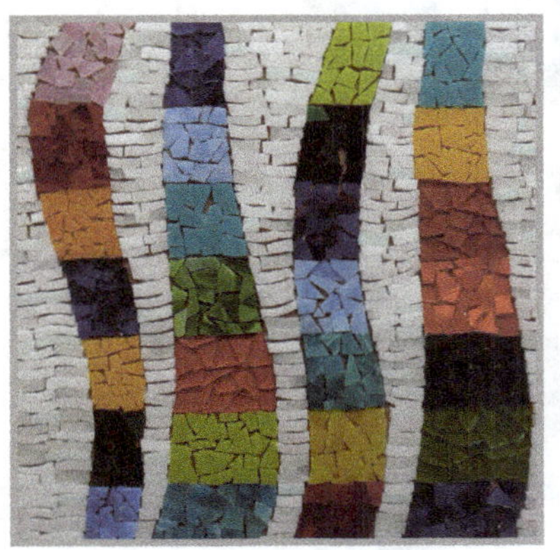

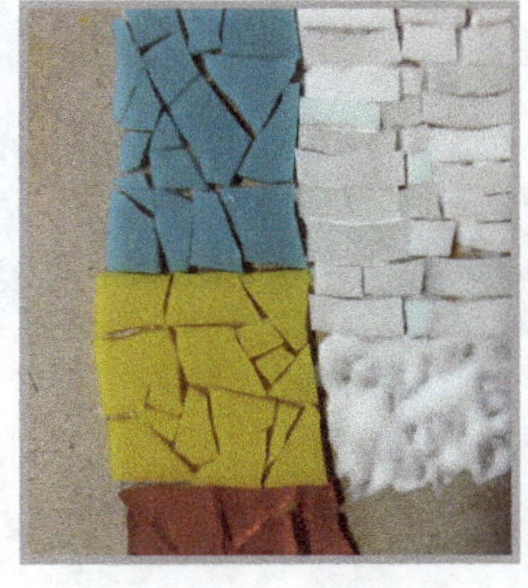

8 When done, leave to dry for 24 hours.

Pattern for the picture: Enlarge on a photocopier by 610% for a full size design

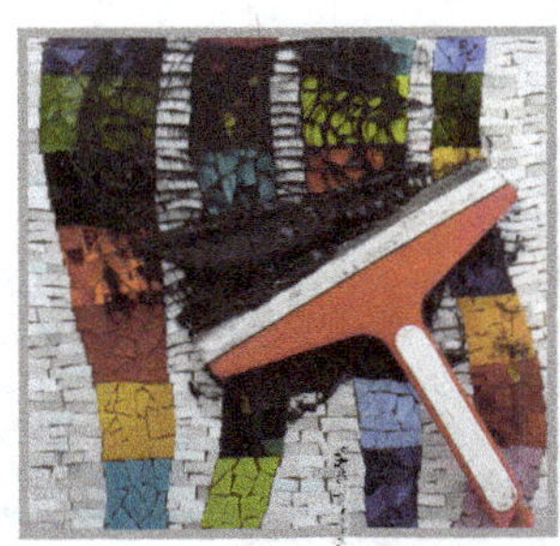

9 Prepare black grout according to manufacturer instructions. Spread over the picture with a squeegee. Douse and clean with a wet rag.

10 I recommend framing the piece to give it a fancier look – I opted for a silver frame.

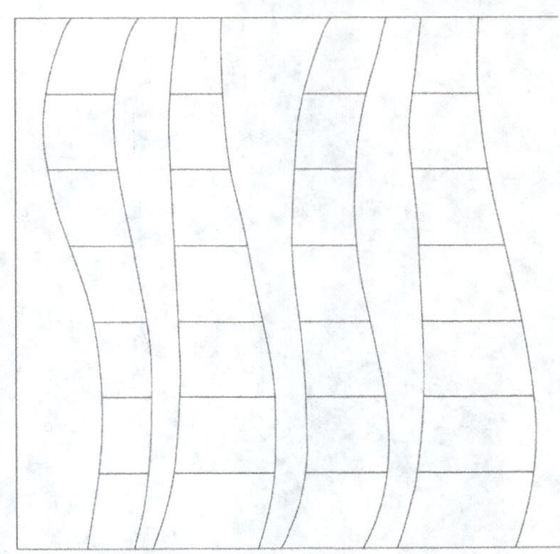

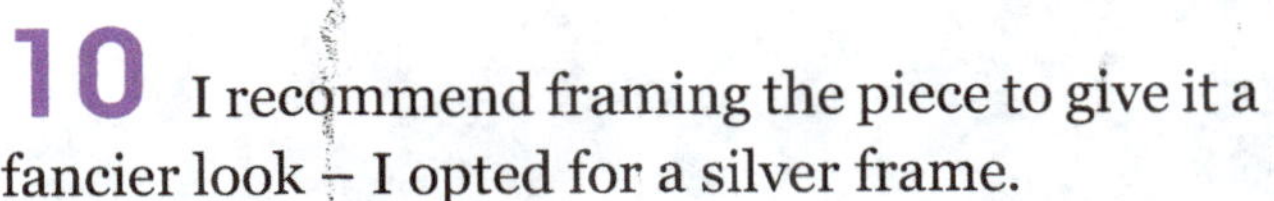

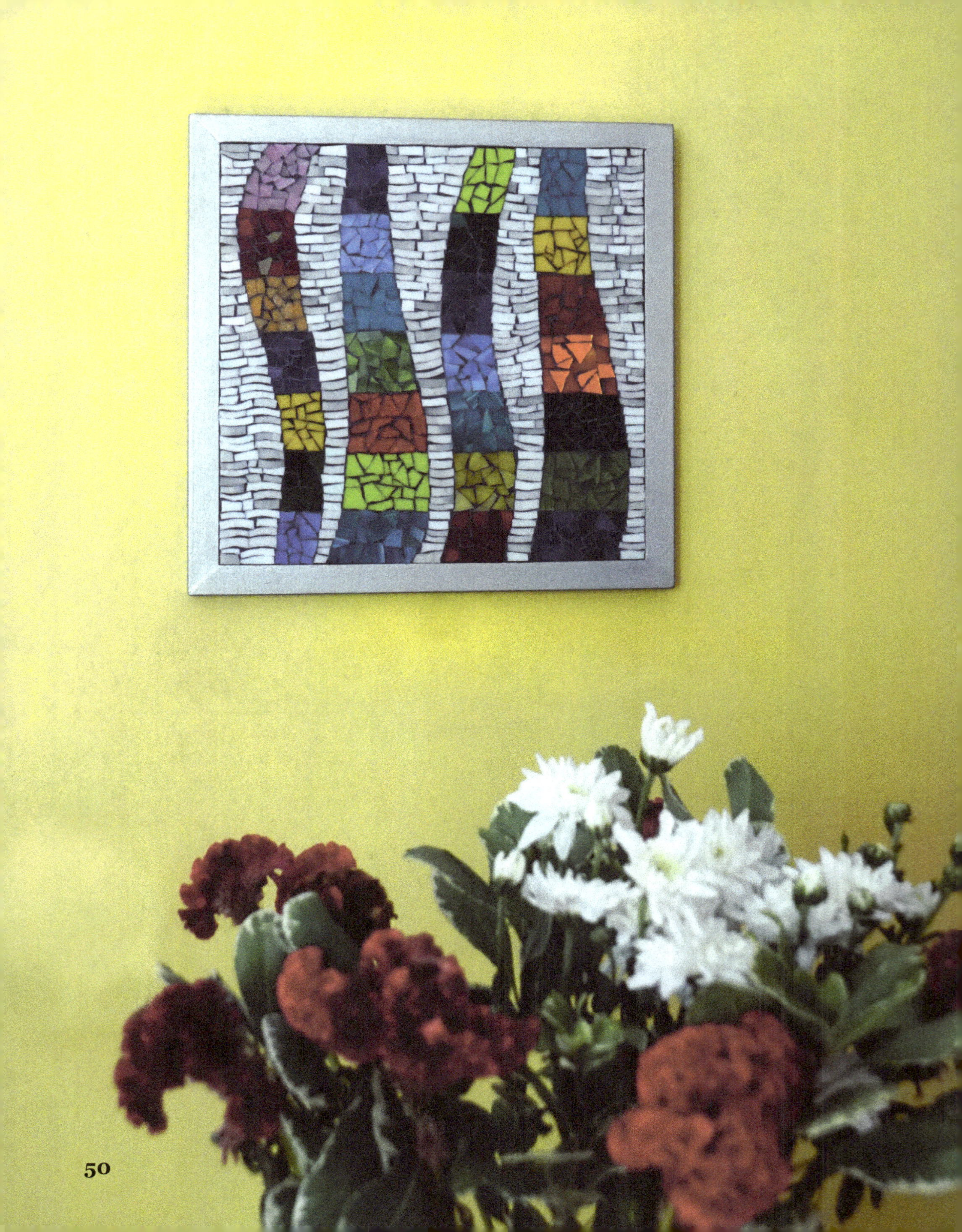

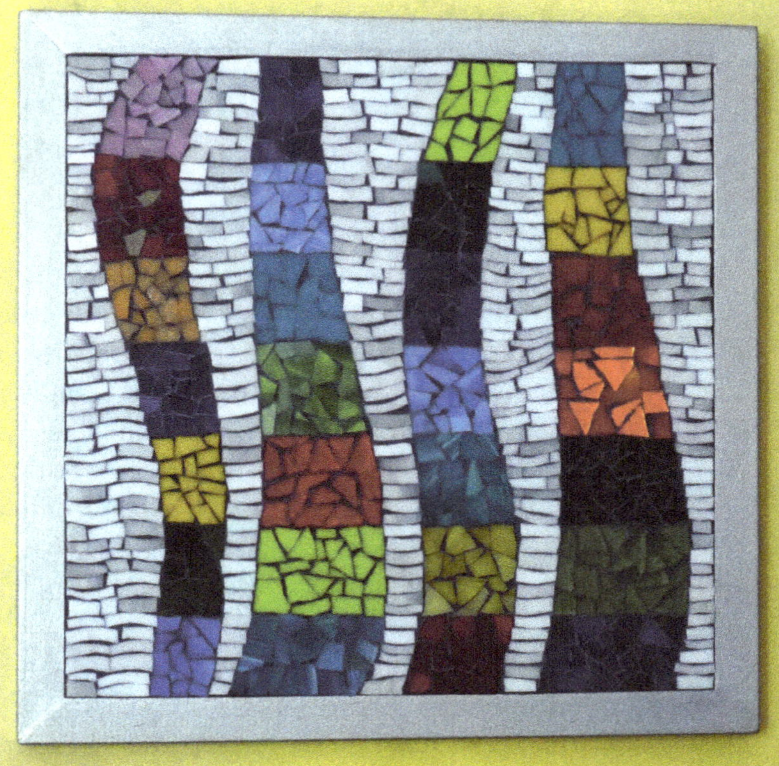

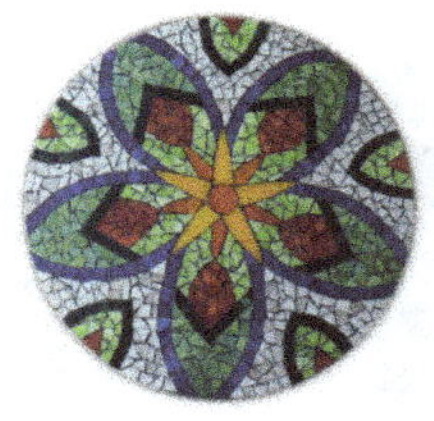

Project No. 10: Mandala

This mandala would look great just about anywhere – you can hang it on the wall as a picture, craft it on a round tray, or paste it onto a turntable, like I did. The pattern is composed of whole pieces cut accurately with the glass cutter, and from randomly cut pieces for filling areas.

Materials:

A round wooden board 38 cm / 15" in diameter

Glass in two shades of blue, two shades of orange, red, two shades of green, and white

Strong white glue

Brush

Pencil

Tracing paper

Nipper

Glass cutter

T-square

Running pliers

Breaker-grozier pliers

Black grout

Grout Equipment: Mixing bowl, water, a wooden stick, rags, gloves

1 Print the mandala pattern and copy it onto the round surface with tracing paper. If the surface area is too large for your printer, print in sections and attach with sticky tape.

2 Cutting the main circle: Cut the circle from the printed design, place the paper on a piece of red glass and mark the circumference. Cut the circle according to the instructions on page 55 and paste to the center of the mandala.

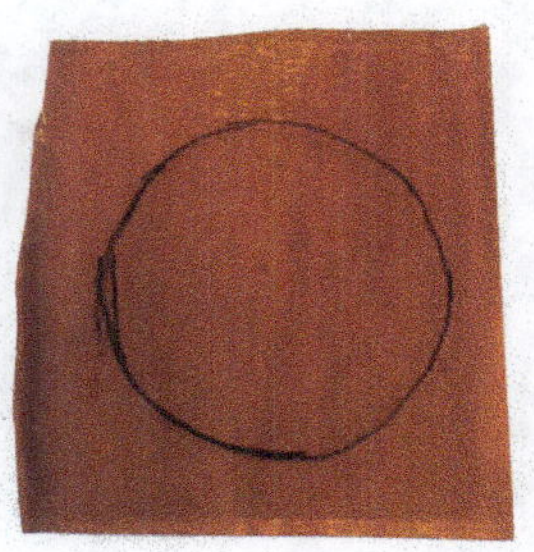

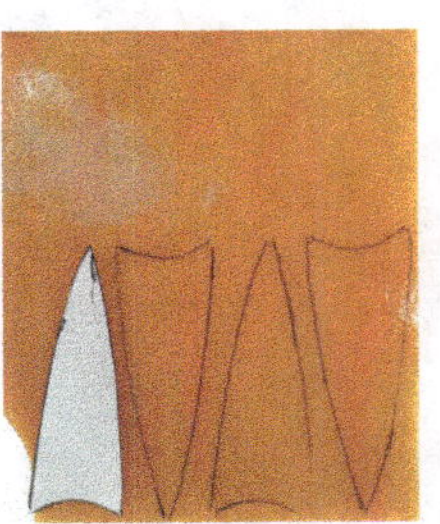

3 Cut one of the long sides of the star and place it on the light orange glass. Mark its shape and cut piece by piece with the glass cutter (see detailed cutting instructions in project no. 7).

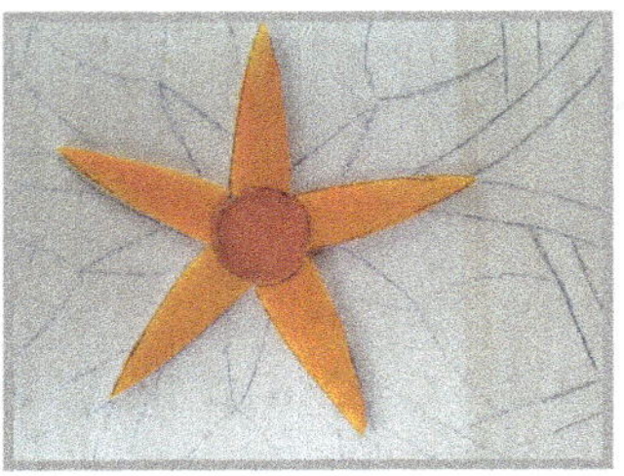
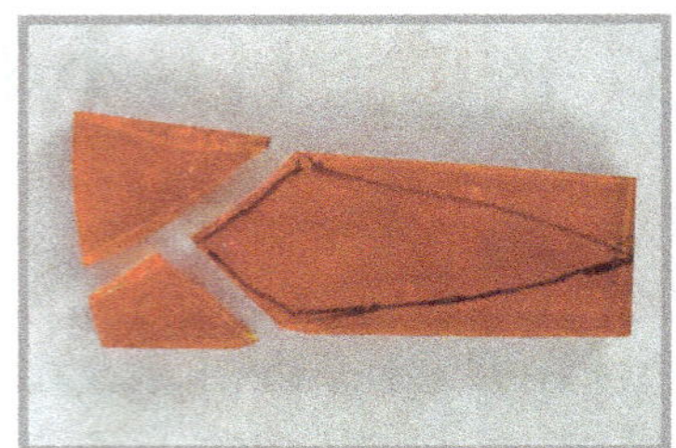
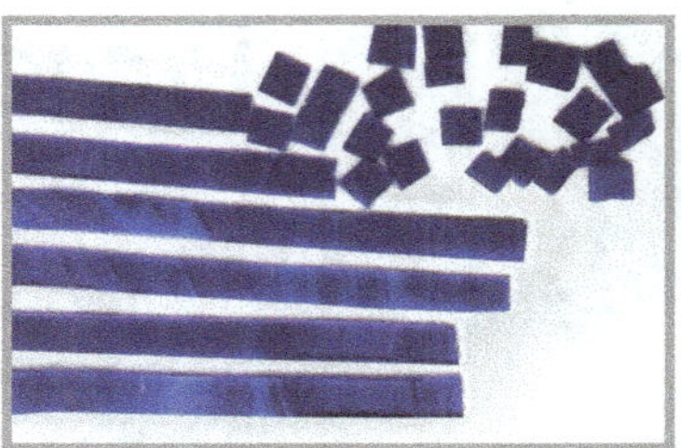

4 Paste the orange star in place at the center of the round board.

5 Using the same method, cut the short sides of the star out of dark orange glass and paste in place.

6 Cut 1.2cm / 0.5" thick blue strips and snap them into rectangles using the nipper.

7 Paste the rectangles in place, according to the pattern, so you'll get 5 blue petals.

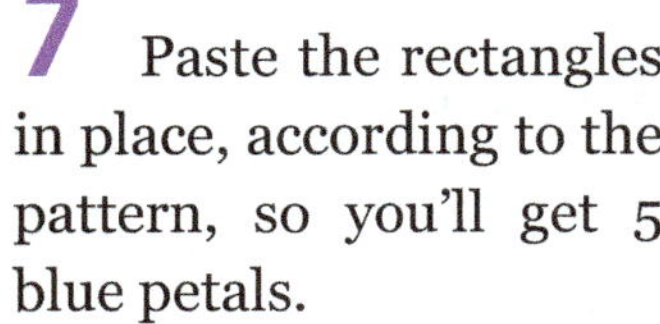

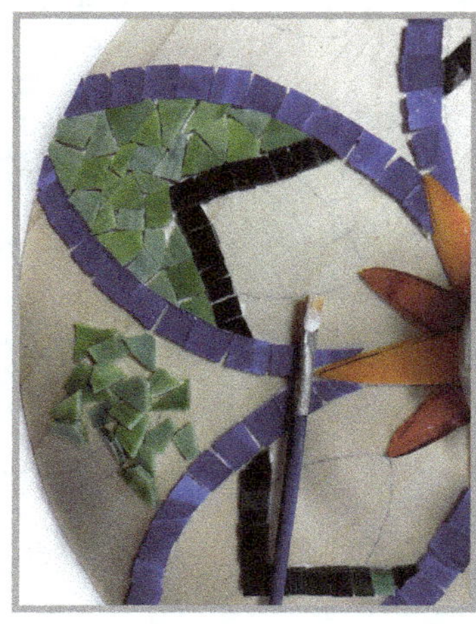

8 Cut dark green glass according to stages 6-7, and paste at the center of each lea

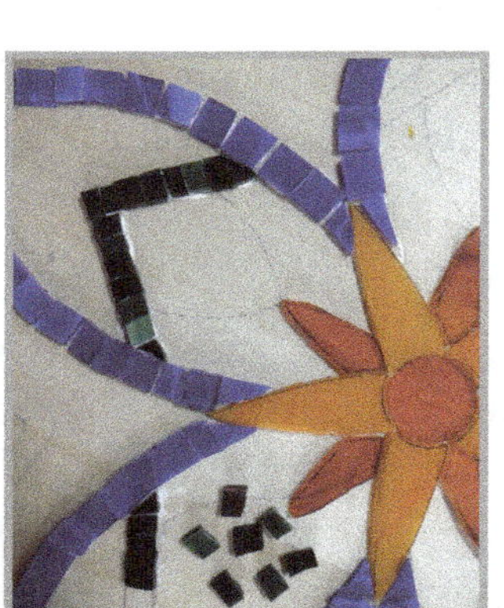

9 Cut green glass into little random pieces and fill the entire top area of each leaf, above the green strip.

10 Cut red glass into small pieces and glue on the leaf on the other side of the green line.

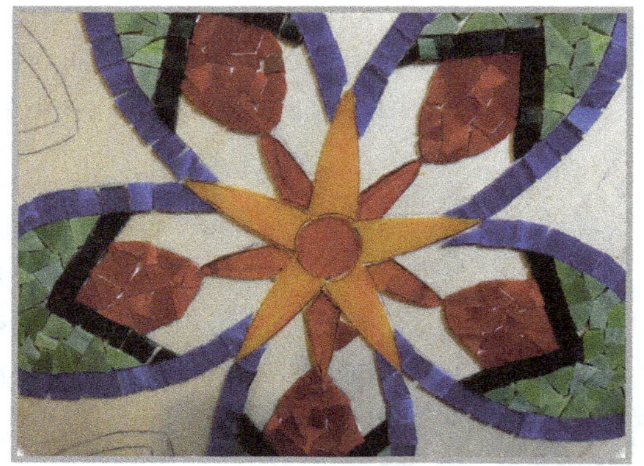

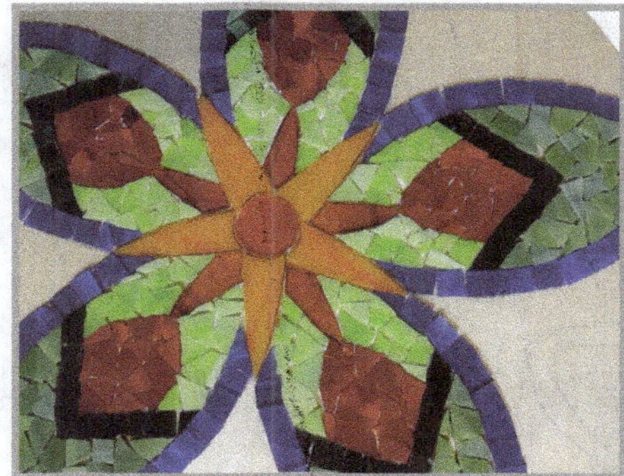

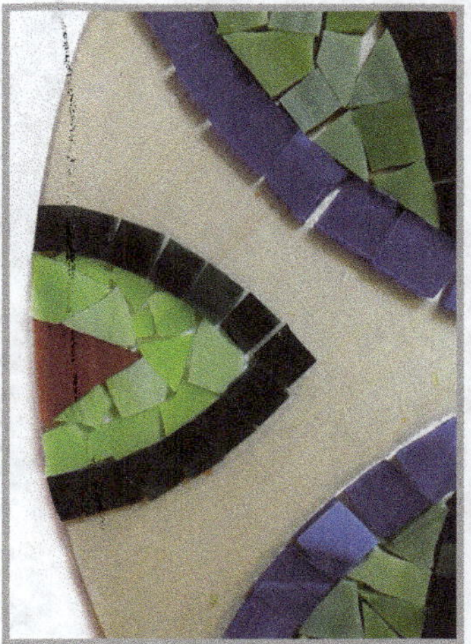

11 Fill in the remaining area in the mandala with light green glass.

13 It's important to cut the red triangle as one piece with two diagonal cuts.

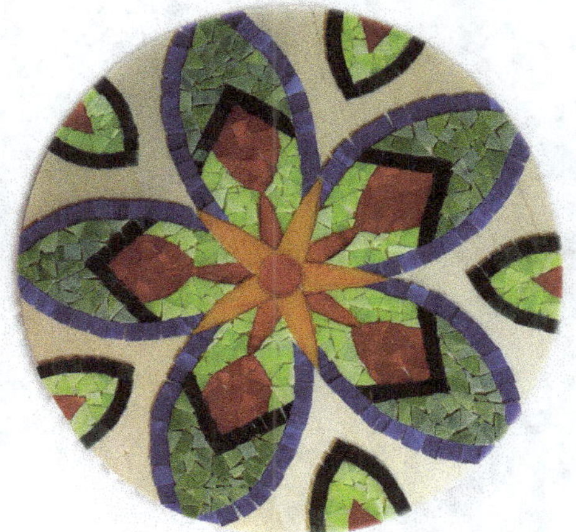

12 Each small triangle at the edges of the mandala will be created from a green contour, a red triangle and light green background.

14 Once the mandala is ready, fill the background with white glass cut into random pieces. Keep the edges straight and smooth. Leave to dry for 24 hours.

15 Prepare black grout according to manufacturer instructions. Spread over the mandala with a small squeegee. Douse and clean with a wet rag. Make sure to keep the finish neat and the edges smooth.

> **Pattern for the mandala:**
> Enlarge on a photocopier by 420% for a full size design

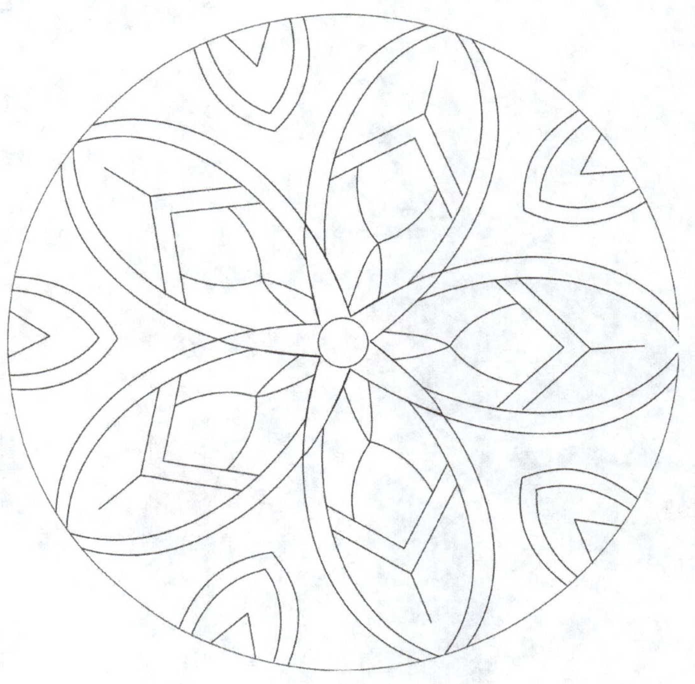

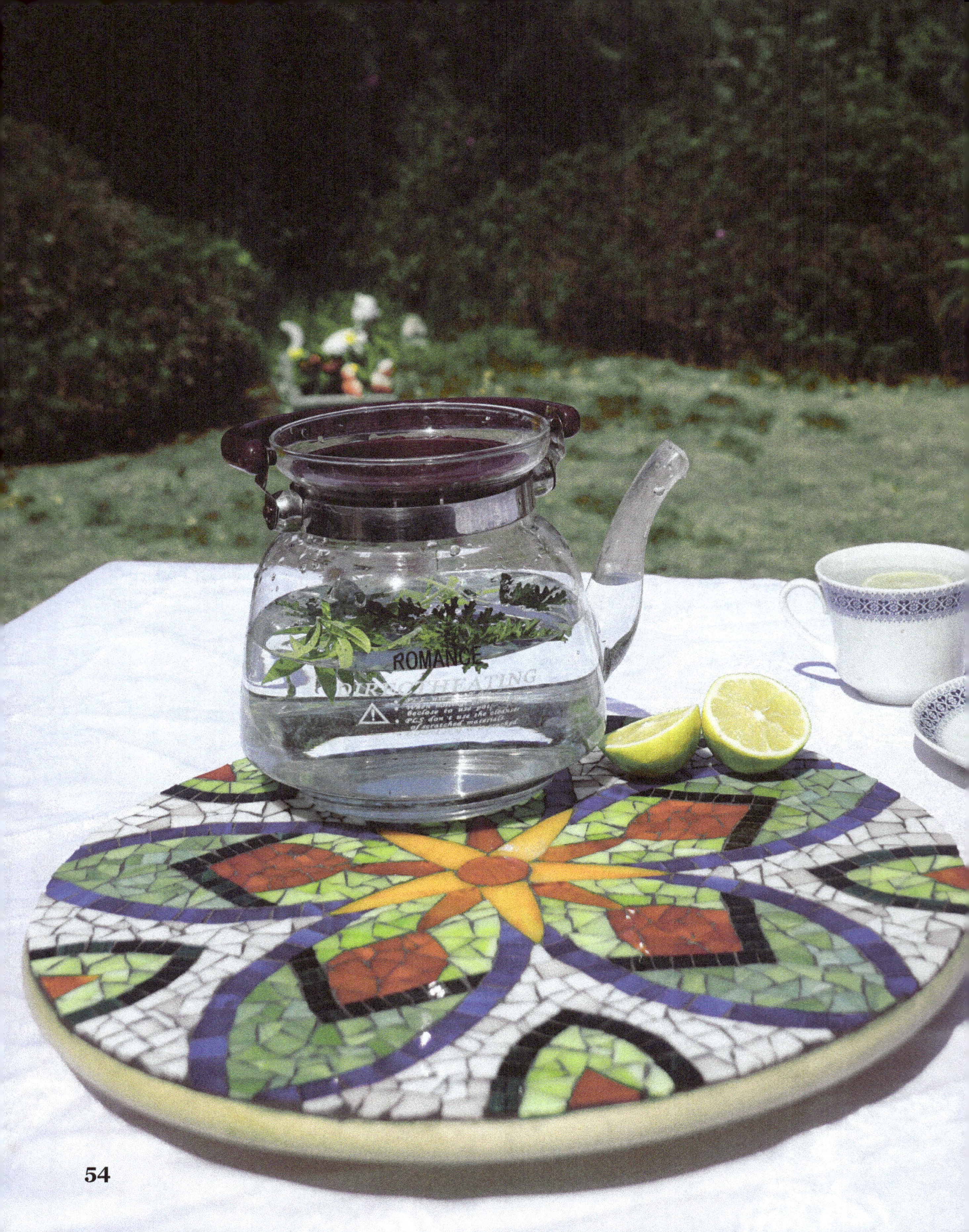
ROMANCE
DIRECT HEATING

Cutting a Glass Circle:

In order to get a circular cut, we need to go step by step. For larger circles, you can use a special circular glass cutter. For small ones, you can use the regular glass cutter.

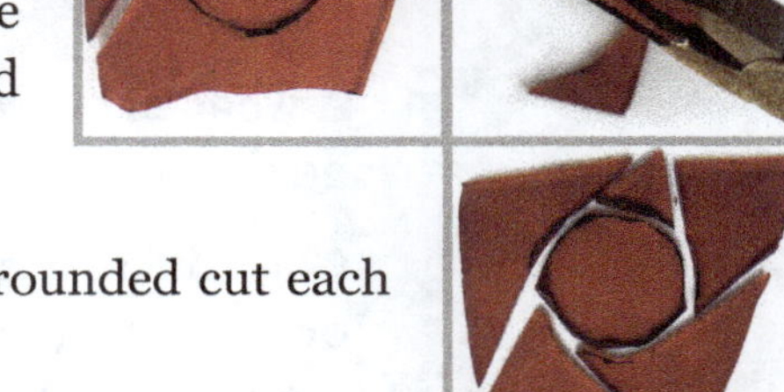

1. Mark the circle over the glass with an appropriate marker. You can cut the circle from the printed pattern or use a bottle cap of the right size.

2. Using the cutter, make a lightly rounded cut in one of the panel corners, from edge to edge. Cut with a breaker-grozier. Note that the straight edge should point upward when you hold the cutter.

3. Repeat in this manner, making a small rounded cut each time until you get a circle.

4. The circle created is usually rough and requires sanding and polishing. The best option would be to use a bench grinder, but there are other methods and at this point there's no need for you to acquire one.
    Using the breaker-grozier, gently cut and round the glass. The cuts should be performed as little "bites", making sure that the rounded side of the pliers is facing upward. Repeat until you've made a nice circle.

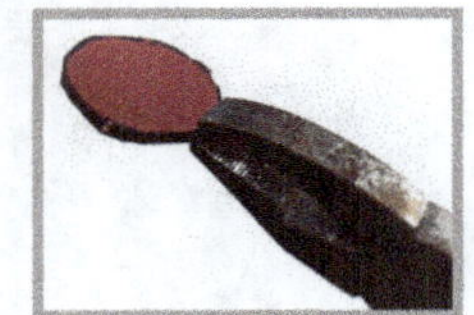

5. Another way to refine the circle is by using a ceramics cutter, hold the tool in opposite way from the way you cut ceramic tiles. Here as well, you should gently "bite" the glass so it won't break.

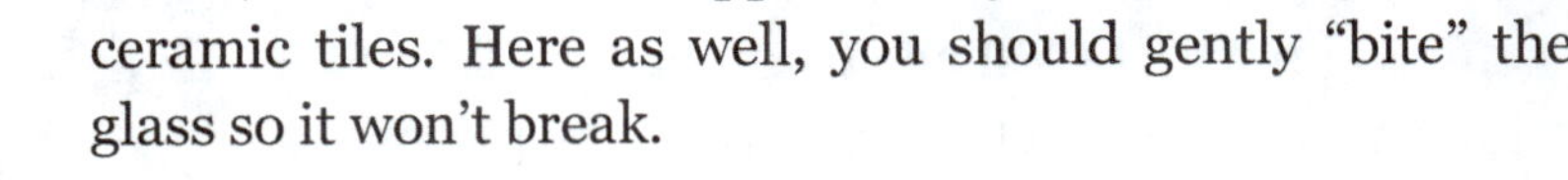

6. When done, you should have a ready-to-use glass circle.

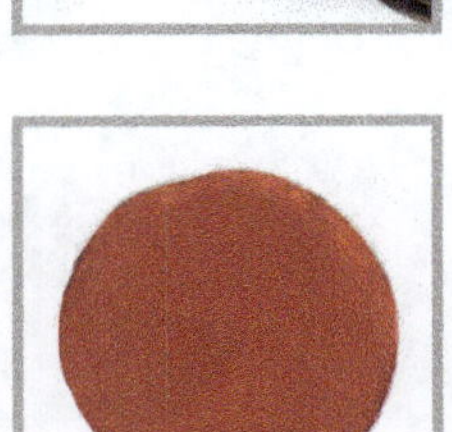

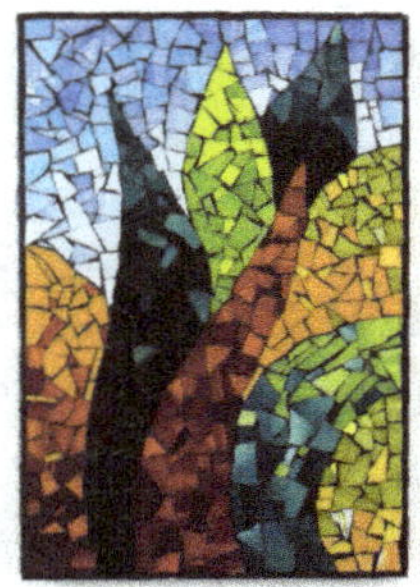

Project No. 11: Color Gradient

The beauty of working with glass is its wealth of colors and shades. This lets us create color gradients, which can be done without buying a huge amount of glass. I recommend using blended and smooth tiles to get good results. Obviously, the more shades we use, the smoother the gradient would be, but we should start with a small number of tiles, in colors we already have in inventory. In this piece, we'll mix transitions from dark to light or from shade to shade to create colorful leaves.

Materials:

A wooden board measuring
20 x 30 cm / 8" x 12"

Glass in several shades of yellow, orange and green, various shades of azure for the background

Strong white glue

Brush

Pencil

Tracing paper

Nipper

Black grout

Grout Equipment: Mixing bowl, water, a wooden stick, rags, gloves

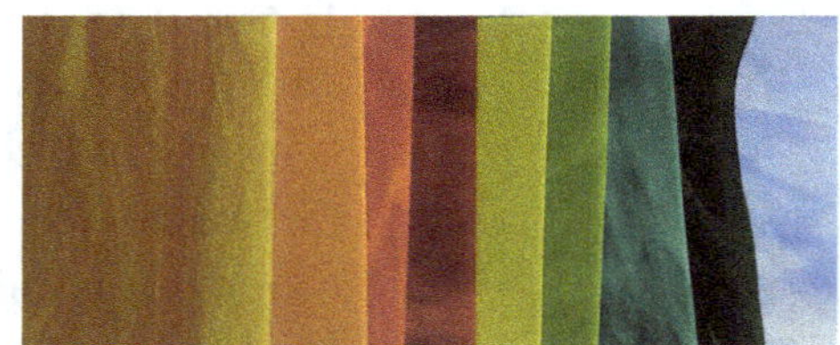

1 Place the pattern over the board and copy with tracing paper.

2 Begin with two shade of green – dark and intermediate. Cut glass into random pieces. Paste the dark glass at the bottom of the leaf, and the light glass at the top. The secret to creating an attractive and interesting gradient is mixing a few pieces of the light glass in the bottom and playing with the ratio to make a gradual transition from dark to light. A harsh transition would give a less than pleasing look.

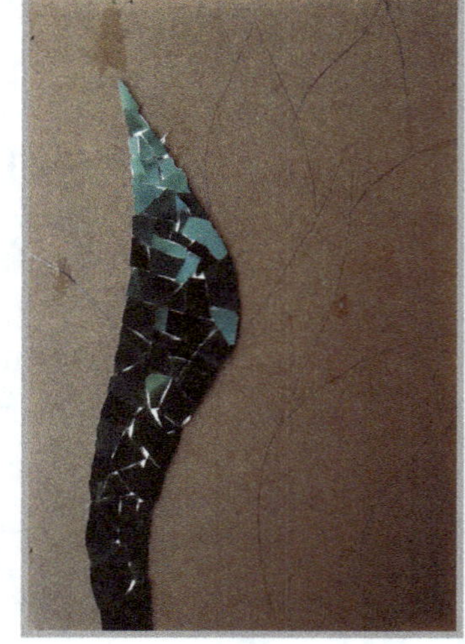

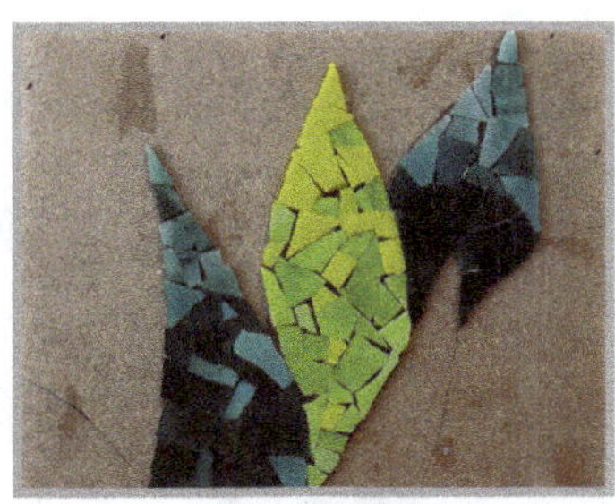

3 In the same manner and with the same colors, paste the top right leaf. Pick a different leaf and create a gradient of two other shades of green. Grass-green transitioning to light green. Again, using the same method. The darker on the bottom and the light on the top, paying attention to the transition between them.

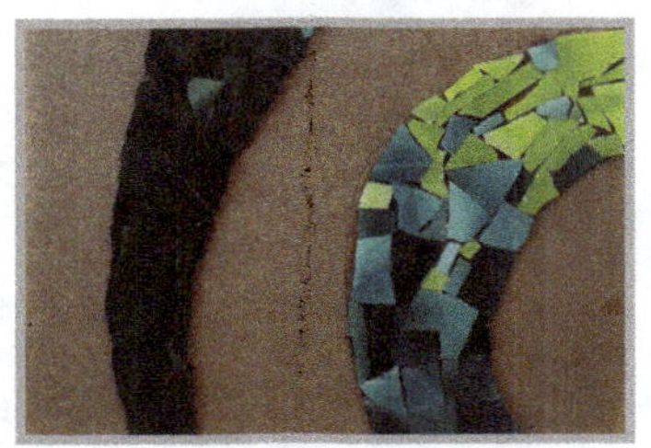

4 3-color gradient: Mix 3 shades of green in one leaf. The two darker ones on the bottom, blended, the light one on top with a few dark spots. When using blended glass, you get a bunch of mid-tones which make for an interesting transition.

5 Using the same method, create a leaf made of red and orange. Pick relatively dark orange, so the transition is harmonious. Paste red on the bottom and orange on top, while mixing orange spots in the red and vice-versa. Use blended red glass to get more color shades.

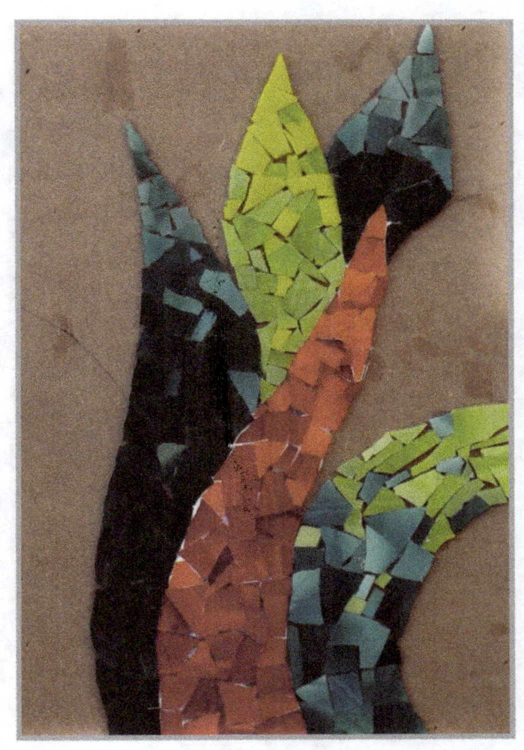

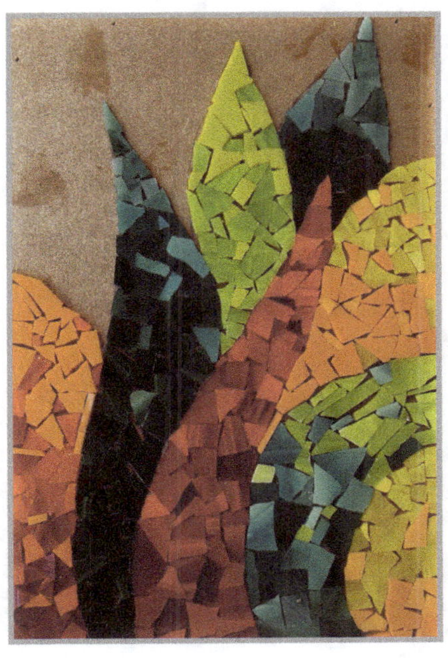

6 Additional shade gradients: From light orange to yellow, from red to light orange (mixing red and two shade of orange). Each gradient creates a different effect.

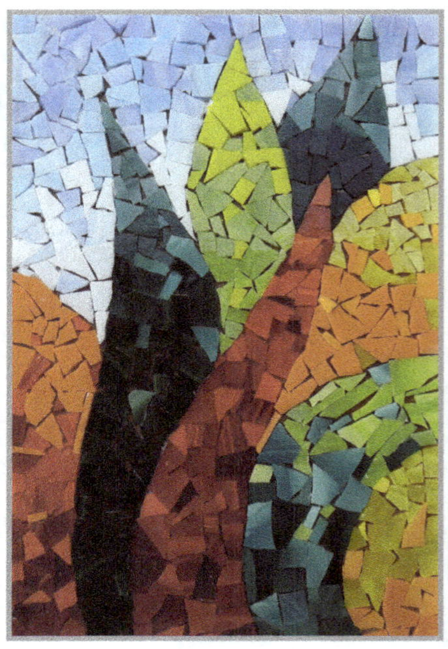

7   Background: The background is made from blended azure glass. I used its dark parts for the top and the light ones for the bottom to create the desired gradient.

I used a 3cm thick wood board, and added a frame of black glass tiles.

When done pasting, leave to dry for 24 hours.

8   Prepare black or dark gray grout (for accentuating the glass) according to manufacturer instructions. Spread with a squeegee. Douse and clean with a wet rag.

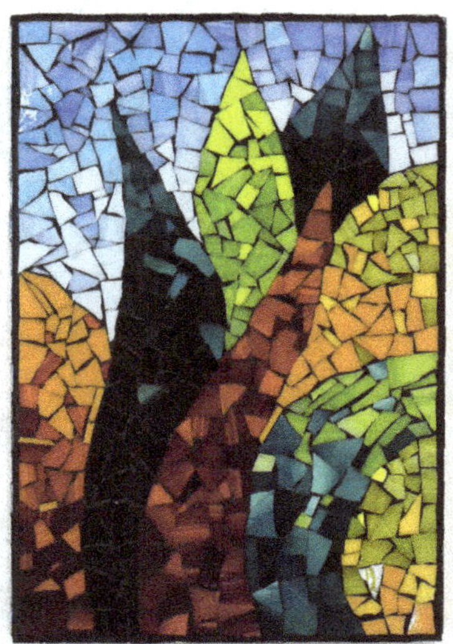

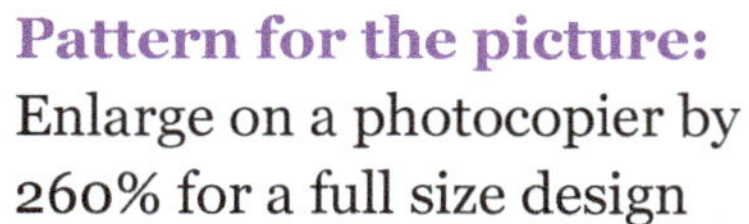

Pattern for the picture:
Enlarge on a photocopier by 260% for a full size design

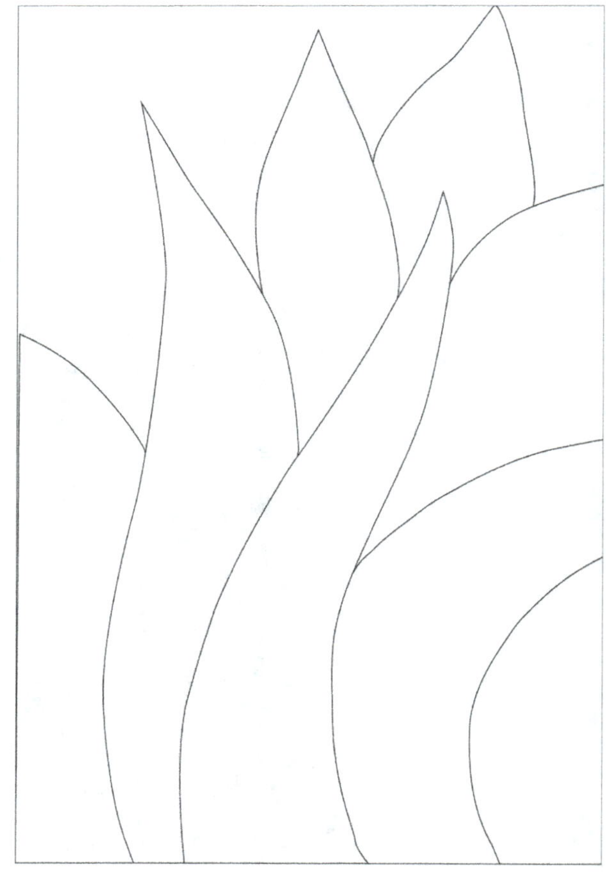

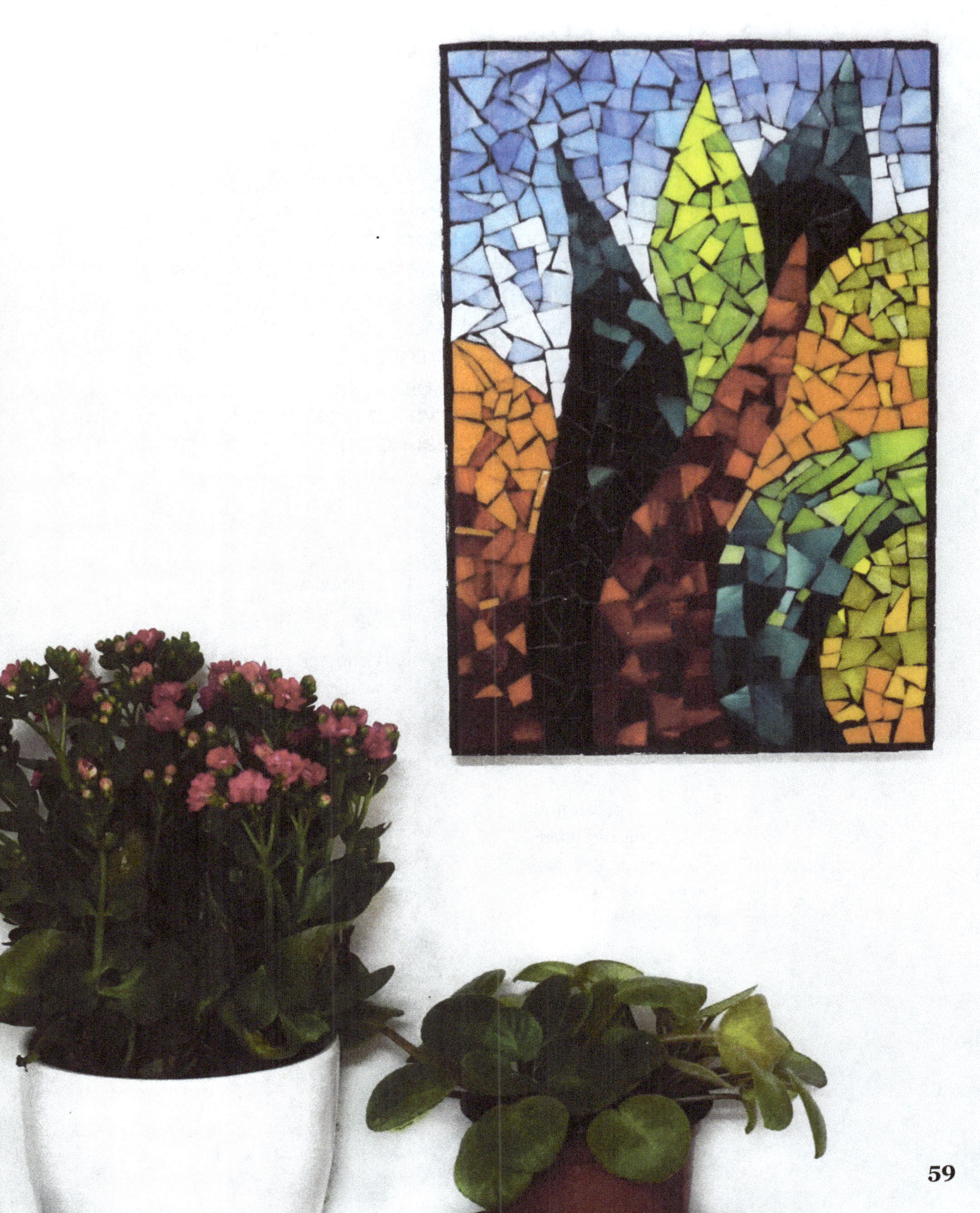

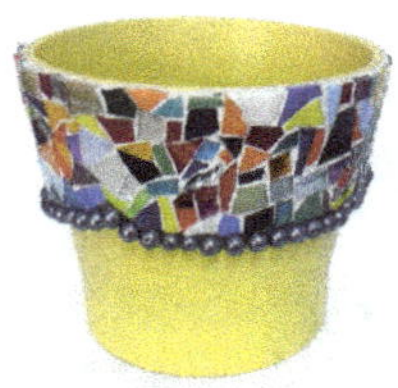

Project No. 12: Leftover Glass Garden Pot

Working with glass produces a lot of leftovers in various sizes. There's no reason to throw these away when you can reuse them, even the tiny ones, for beautiful works of art. The small pieces can be kept together in one receptacle for this type of work, or in covered disposable cups for each color.

I chose a colored flowerpot and pasted a colorful pattern to a portion of it, while using its natural color.

Note the glue – for a ceramic piece that you can leave outside, it's better to use tile glue. To give it a nice finish, I decorated with grey beads I took off an old necklace.

Materials:

A small colored garden pot

Leftover glass in various shades

Tile glue

Wooden stick

Pencil

Nipper

Screwdriver

Off-white or beige grout

Grout Equipment: Mixing bowl, water, a wooden stick, rags, gloves

1 Gather a large amount of leftover colored glass in various sizes. You can use pieces of glass tiles or leftovers from glass panels.

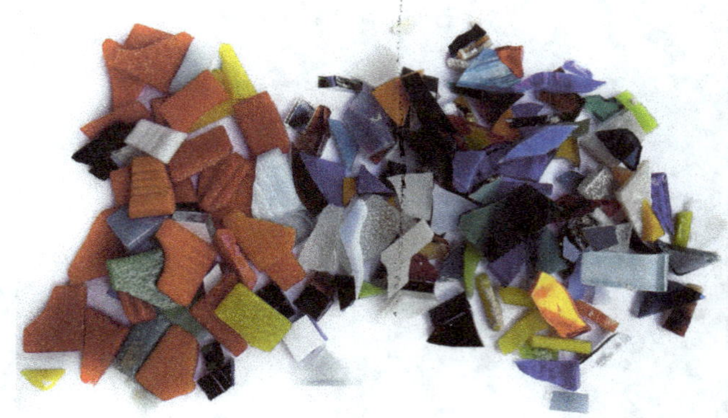

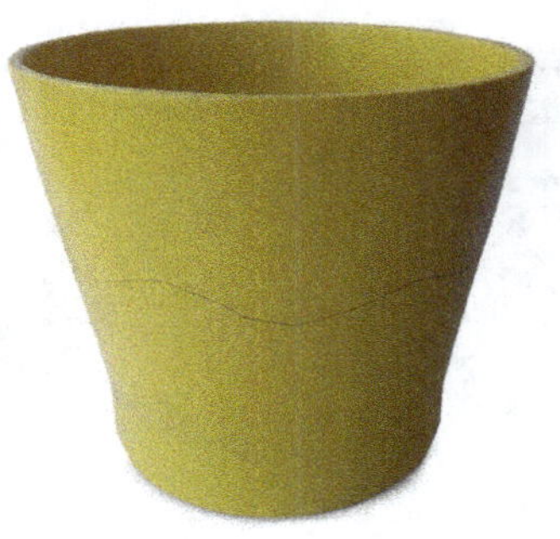

2 Paint a wave pattern on the colored pot all the way around, in the desired height (one half or one third the way up).

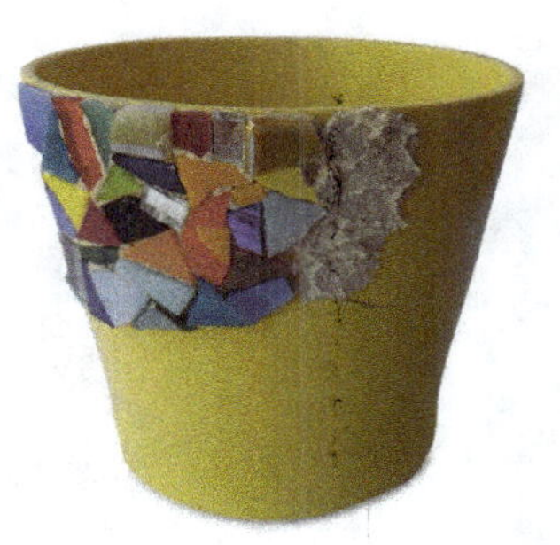

3 Paste the glasses on the pot with tile glue. For convenience, spread the glue over a small area and fill it with glass before repeating. It's essential to keep the top edge Smooth and with minimal gaps. Keep your work neat and tidy. You can add a decorative strip for the finish – I opted for round gray beads. When done, leave to dry for 24 hours.

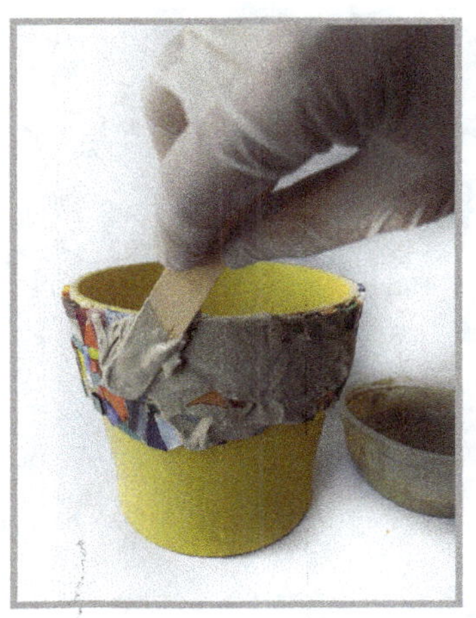

4 Prepare grout according to manufacturer instructions and spread over the pot. It's a good idea to choose grout close in color to that of the tile glue. Clean thoroughly with a wet rag.

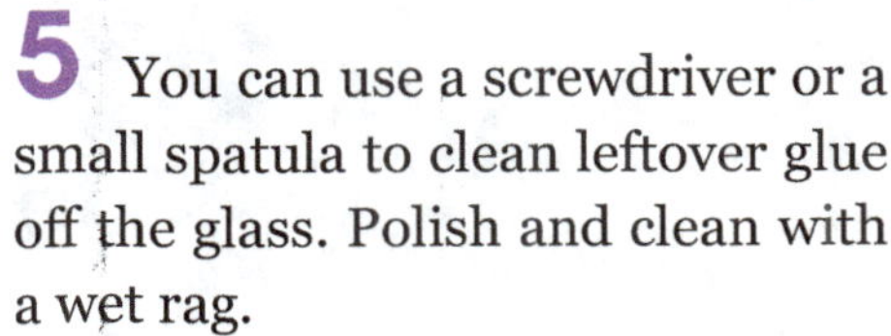

5 You can use a screwdriver or a small spatula to clean leftover glue off the glass. Polish and clean with a wet rag.

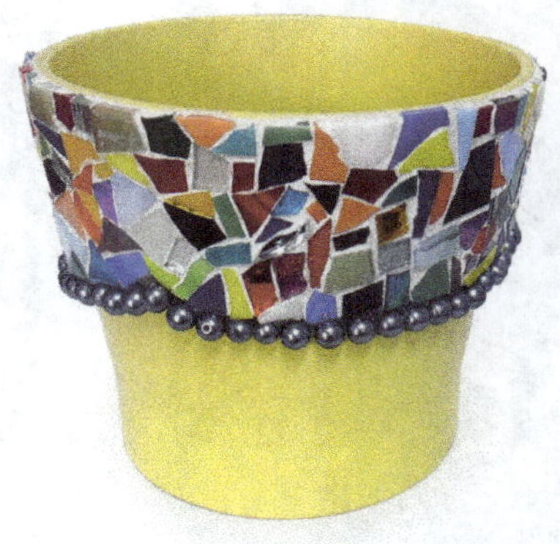

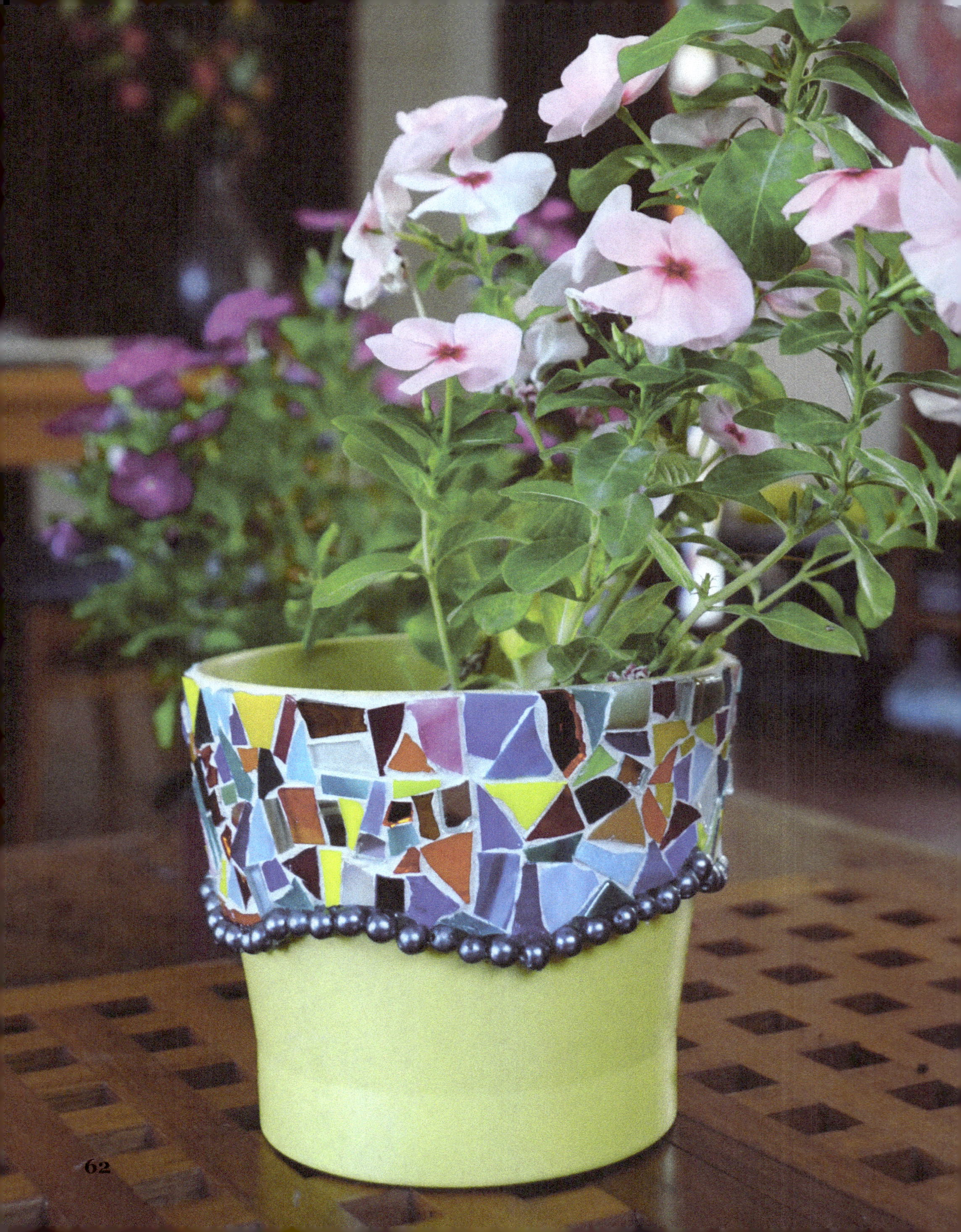

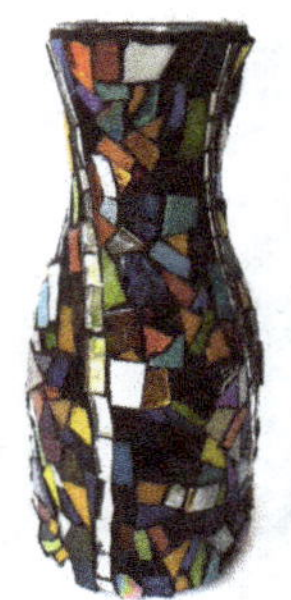

Project No. 13: Vase of Leftover Glass and Mirror

Glass can be pasted to various materials: Wood, metal, stone and even other glass. This glass vase is crafted from leftover glass and strips of mirror circling around it, adding interest and giving it a fancier look. You can place it in the middle of the table with a single flower or gift it to a loved one.

Materials:

A smooth glass vase

Leftover glass in various shades

Mirror

Glass adhesive

Gloves

A wooden stick

Nipper

Glass cutter

T-square

Running pliers

Off-white or beige grout

Grout Equipment: Mixing bowl, water, a wooden stick, rags, gloves

1 Prepare a smooth glass vase with no handles.

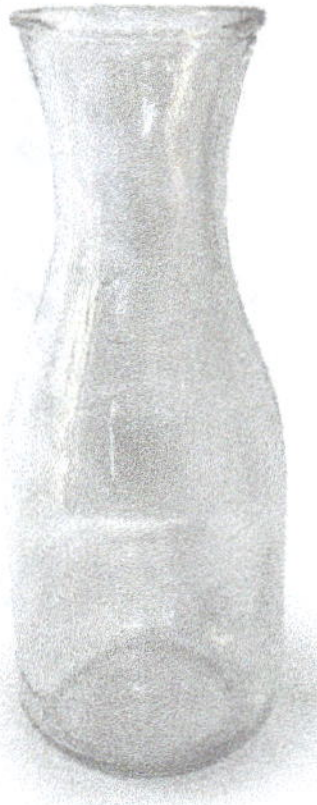

2 Gather a large amount of leftover colored glass, in various sizes and colors. Cut a mirror into thin strips using the glass cutter, and snap into rectangles (see detailed instructions for cutting).

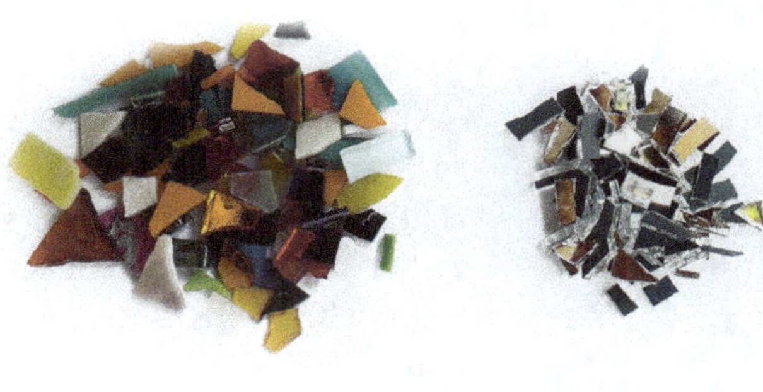

3 Wear gloves – Working with glass adhesive should always be done with gloves. Glue several rounded lengthwise strips of mirror pieces. You can spread the glass adhesive right on the mirror. Note that it dries quickly, so you should keep the spread areas small. You can use a pencil but not a marker for the line, since the glass is clear and will show it on the outside.

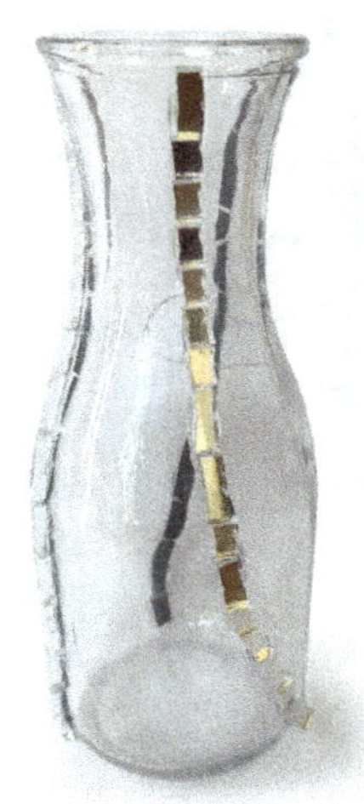

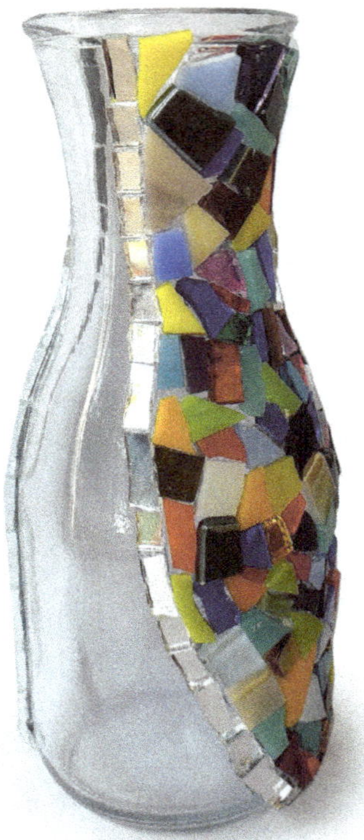

4 Paste the colored glass between the mirror strips. Maintain a straight finish on the top of the vase. Use the nipper if necessary to adjust the pieces. When done, leave to dry for 24 hours.

5 Prepare black grout according to manufacturer instructions and coat the vase. You can use a scraper rather than your hands. Clean thoroughly with a wet rage and polish.

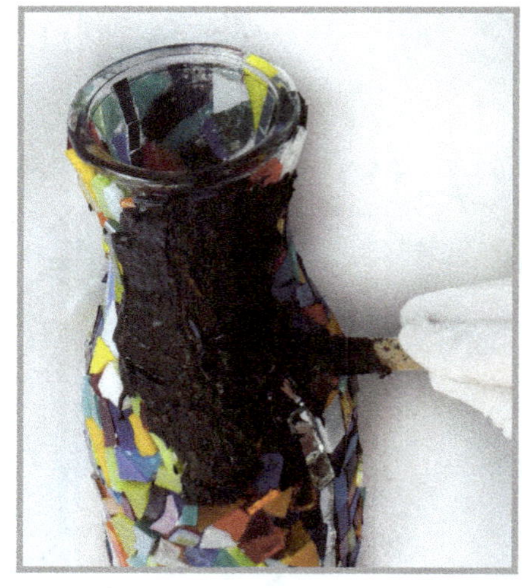

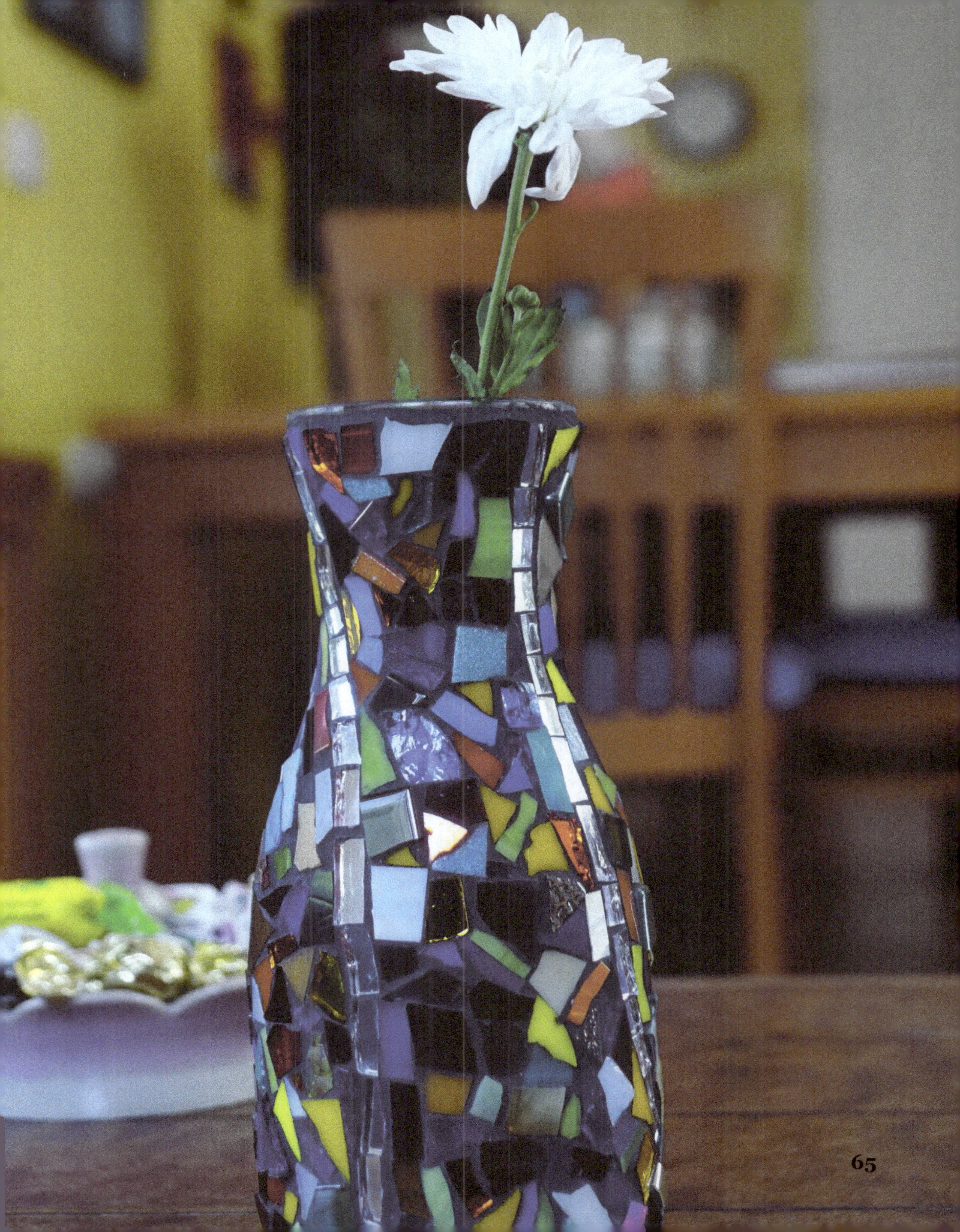

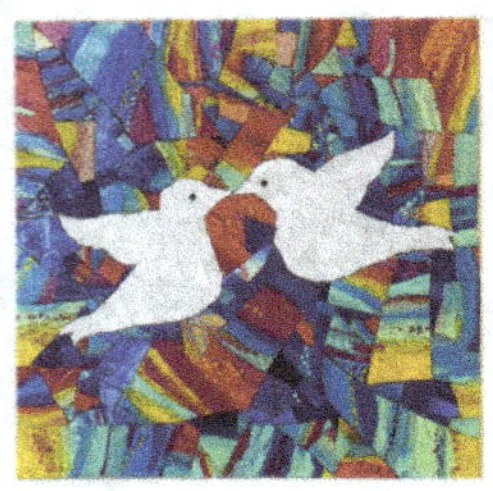

Project No. 14: Creating Colored Glass – by Yourself!

Colored glass is expensive, I know. You also have to collect numerous colors to add diversity to your work. So, I want to teach you an easy, simple and cheap method of creating your own colored glass. You don't need a kiln or any expensive instruments. All you need is… nail polish! You can get it in a wide variety of colors and paint the glass or draw patterns on it. You don't need great talent, and you can even get your kids to join the fun.

Prepare a 3mm thick clear glass panel – you can get it at your local hardware store. Collect your old nail polish bottles and buy new ones in shades you don't have. It's advised that you paint in a well-ventilated environment, since nail polish has a very potent odor.

You can integrate the entire panel in your work, but can also use it for a cheerful, colorful background like this bird picture.

I made this picture of birds on canvas. In this case there is no need for grout, but make sure that the canvas is stretched tight enough to hold the glass.

Materials for Making Colored Glass:

Clear 3mm glass

Various colors of nail polish

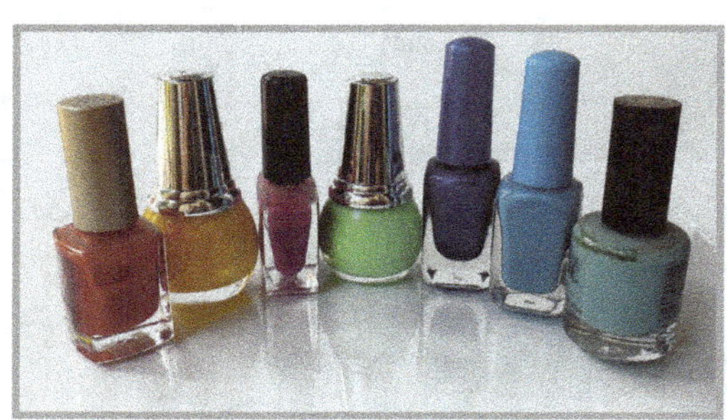

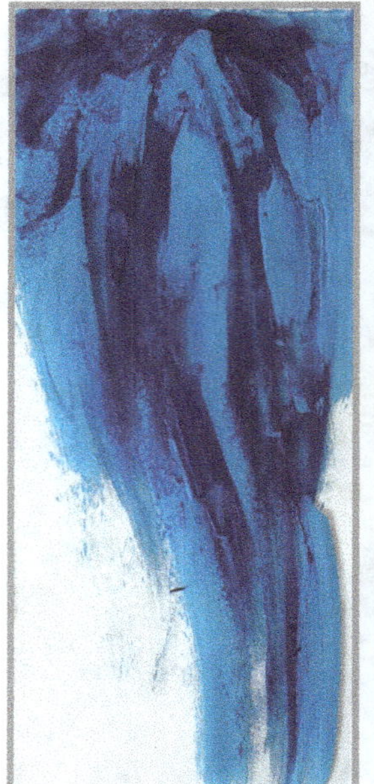

1 It's recommended that you start with a small panel of clear 3 mm glass. Pick a color or two and begin painting the glass in stripes.

2 You can add some dots using the nail polish's brush.

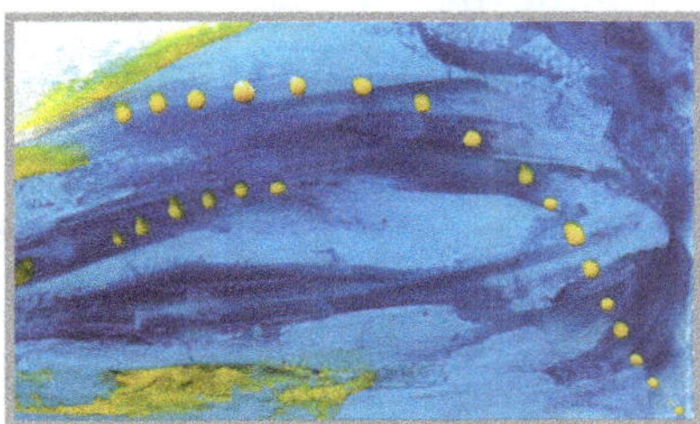

3 And more dots, together with other colors. Remember that you're not creating a masterpiece, just coloring glass in various colors, which you will use for crafting the mosaic.

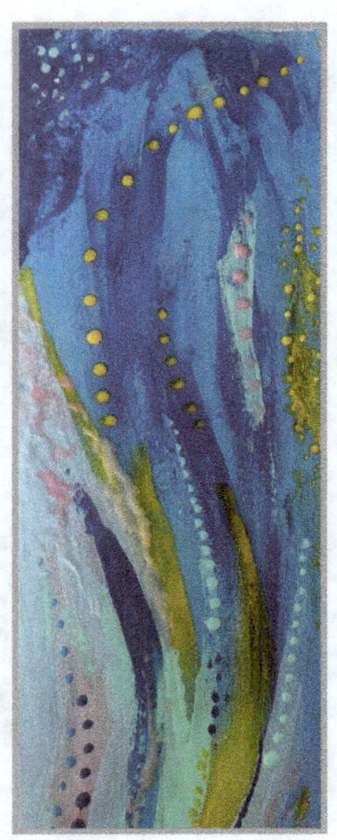

4 Adding a few dots can create a flower, and you can also add glittery nail polish. Leave for at least 1 hour, until the glass is completely dry.

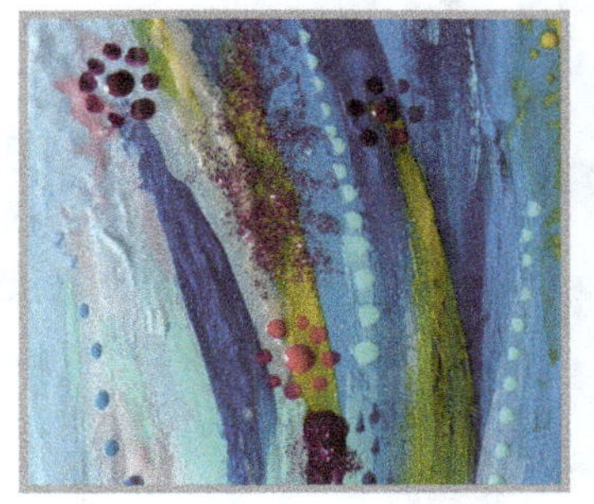

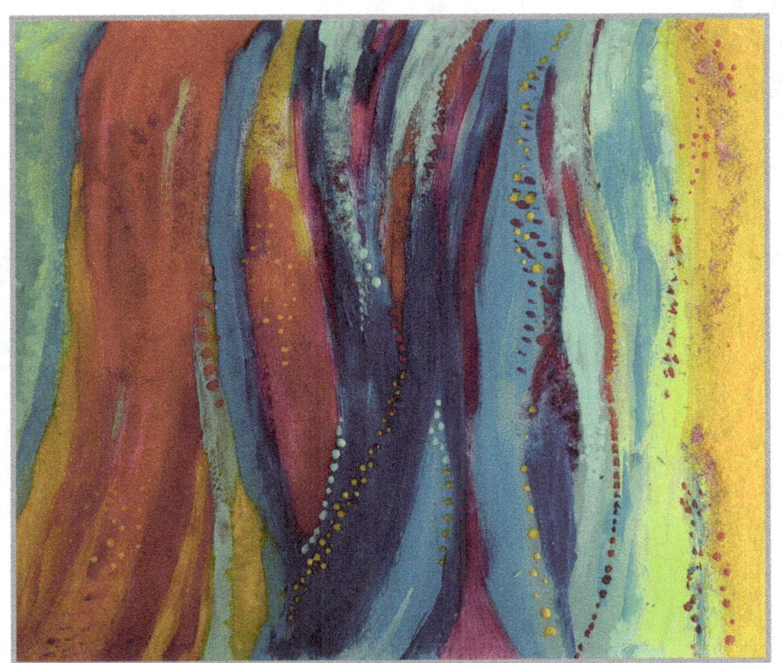

Picture Materials:

Canvas or wooden square measuring 29 x 29 cm / 11.5" x 11.5"

Acrylic paint (if desired)

White glass (one-sided seashell texture is fine)

Polish-colored glass

Strong white glue

Brush

Light brown acrylic color for the surface

Nipper

Glass cutter

Running pliers

1 Color the surface with Acrylic paint in the desired color and let it dry. Copy the bird's pattern after the color is completely dry. You can paint the birds white before pasting the glass.

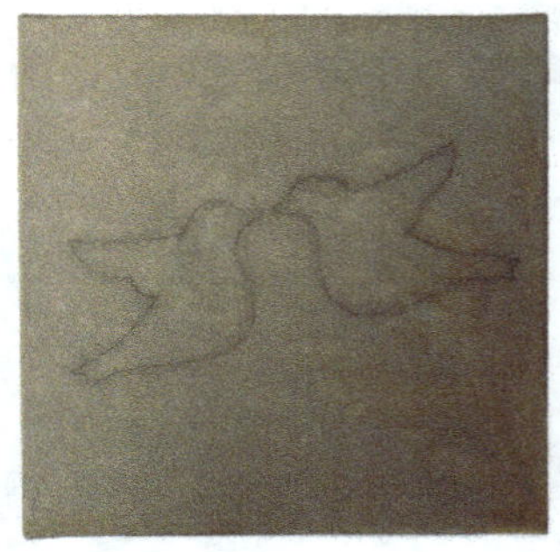

2 Cut white glass into little pieces. It's advised that you use glass with seashell texture on one side, so you get several shades. Glue black beads for eyes.

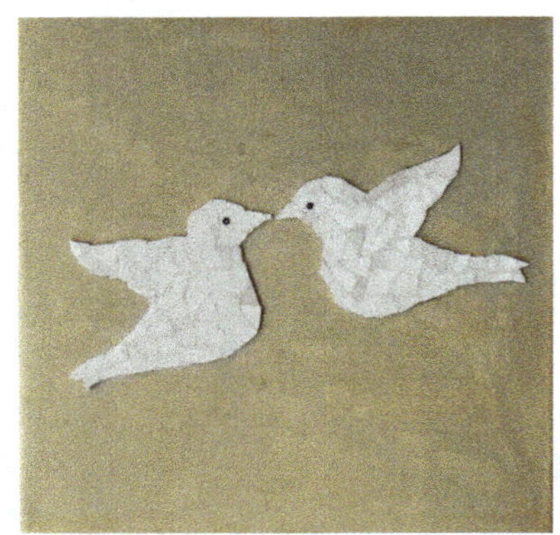

(Since I wanted a smooth surface for the bird body, I filled the gaps with white grout using a gentle brush. You can paste the glasses close together or paint the bird's area in white before pasting.)

3 Using the glass cutter, cut the panel into various sized pieces and continue to break some of them into even smaller pieces with the nipper. Use both large and small pieces for the work.

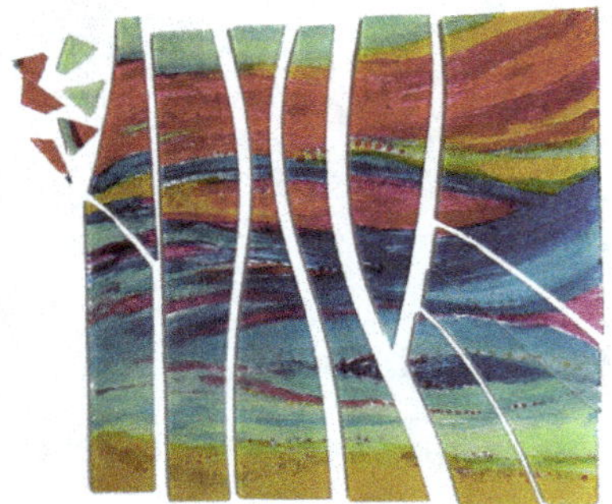

Important! The colored glass should be cut from its smooth, opposite side.

4 Paste the colored glass around the birds. Begin at the edges, integrate large pieces of colored glass and insert little pieces between them to cover everything. Fit them as tight as you can. Continue until the picture is complete. You can mix in smooth glass if necessary.

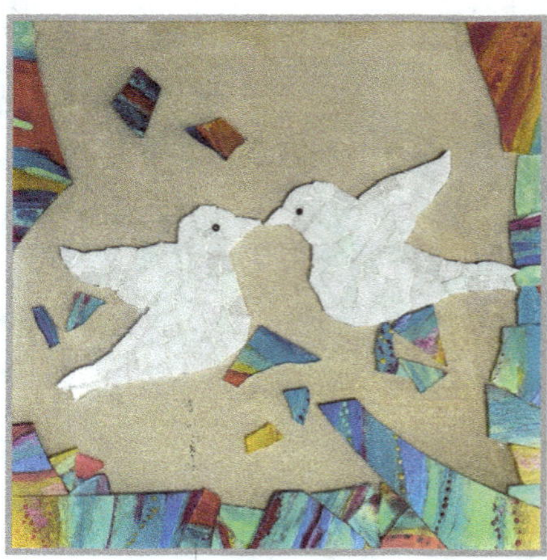

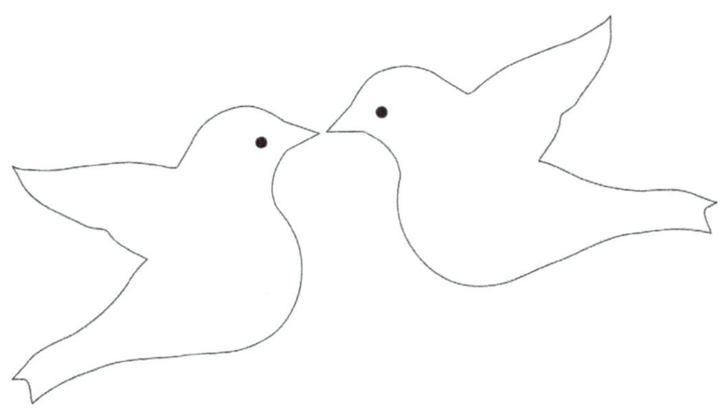

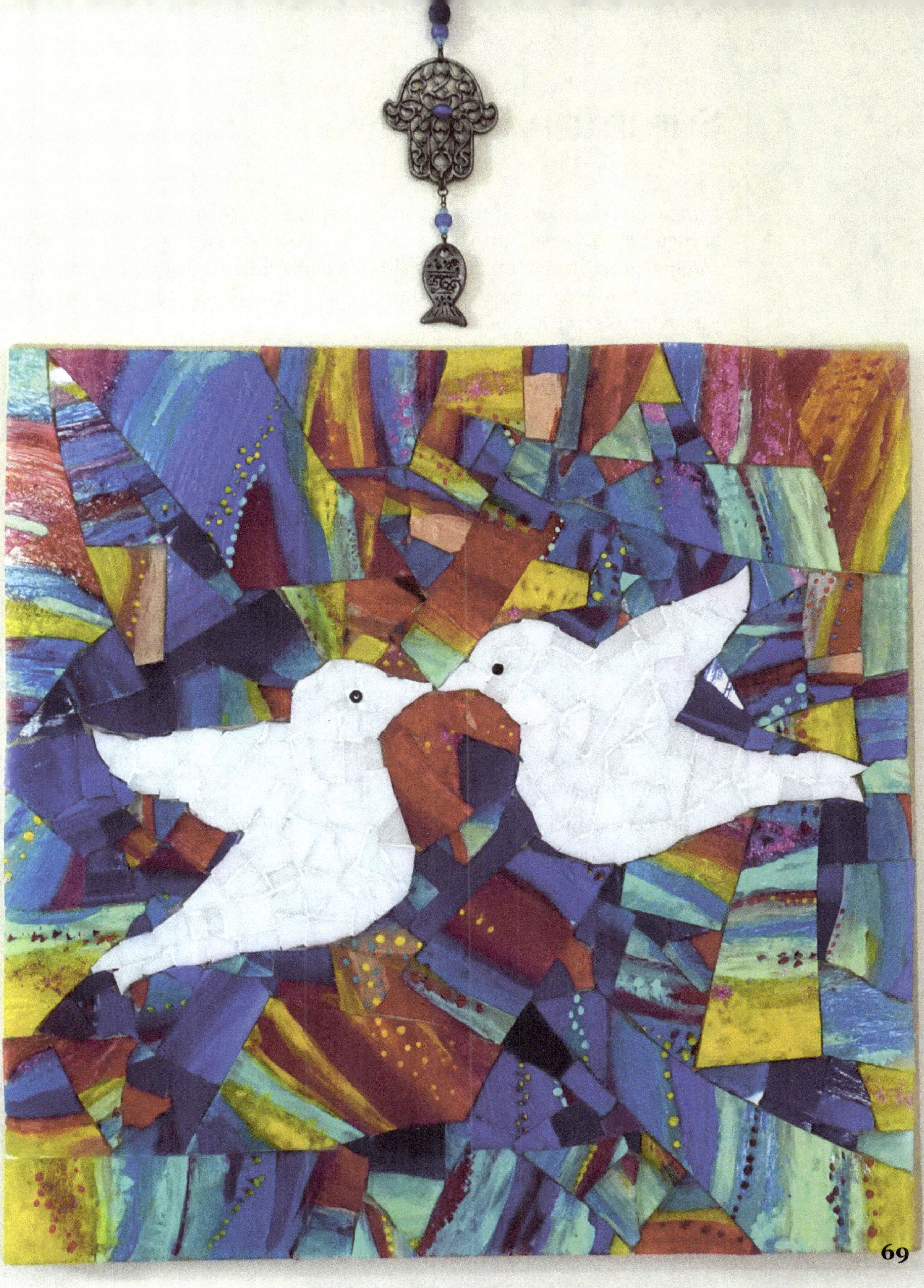

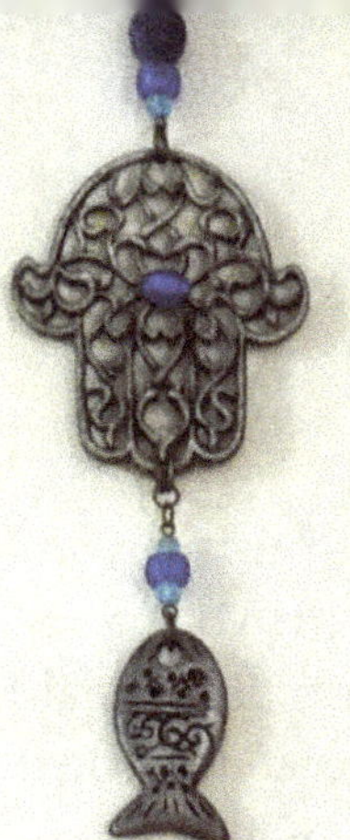

Summary

I hope I've managed to infect you with some of my love for mosaics, and particularly glass work. If you've created a mosaic or two using glass, you've surely realized its charm. The wealth of colors, infinite shades, its gloss and spark... make every piece glow. You don't have to undertake a huge piece – you can go for as small as you like.

In this book, we've had a taste of working with this magnificent medium. If you've enjoyed it and wish to delve deeper, I encourage you to acquire better gear, use a grinding machine for nicer, smoother shapes, learn to work with Smalti, and of course make sure you have a myriad of shades to work with.

We've learned to use glass tiles, both whole and cut. We've learned to cut glass into different shapes: Random cuts or straight nipper cuts, and using the glass cutter to create strips or more complex shapes. We've glued colored glass on various materials – wood, metal, canvas and glass.

We've acquainted ourselves with creating shades while using glass and finally – a unique and easy technique for creating colored glass ourselves. I highly advise you try and experiment with this – I'm sure you'll be surprised by how well it turns out.

As always, it's essential to maintain safety precautions, as getting injured is very easy when working with glass.

All project examples presented in the book are at your disposal. You can print and magnify them.

I'd love to hear your thoughts on the book and see your work.

Keep your spirit creative!

Yours,

Sigalit Eshet

There is a bonus for you. All the patterns that are showed in this book, are available in a pdf file, for your use:

Just type **http://bit.ly/2jk8UrZ** in your browser and get it.

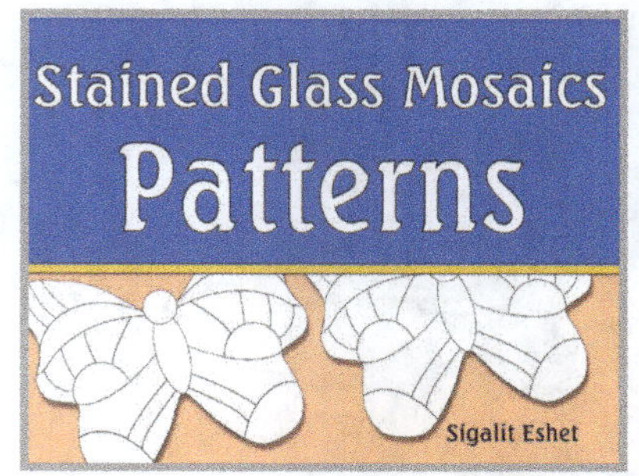

If from some reason you can't get the file, please email me and I will mail it to you:

Sigalit@sigalitart.net

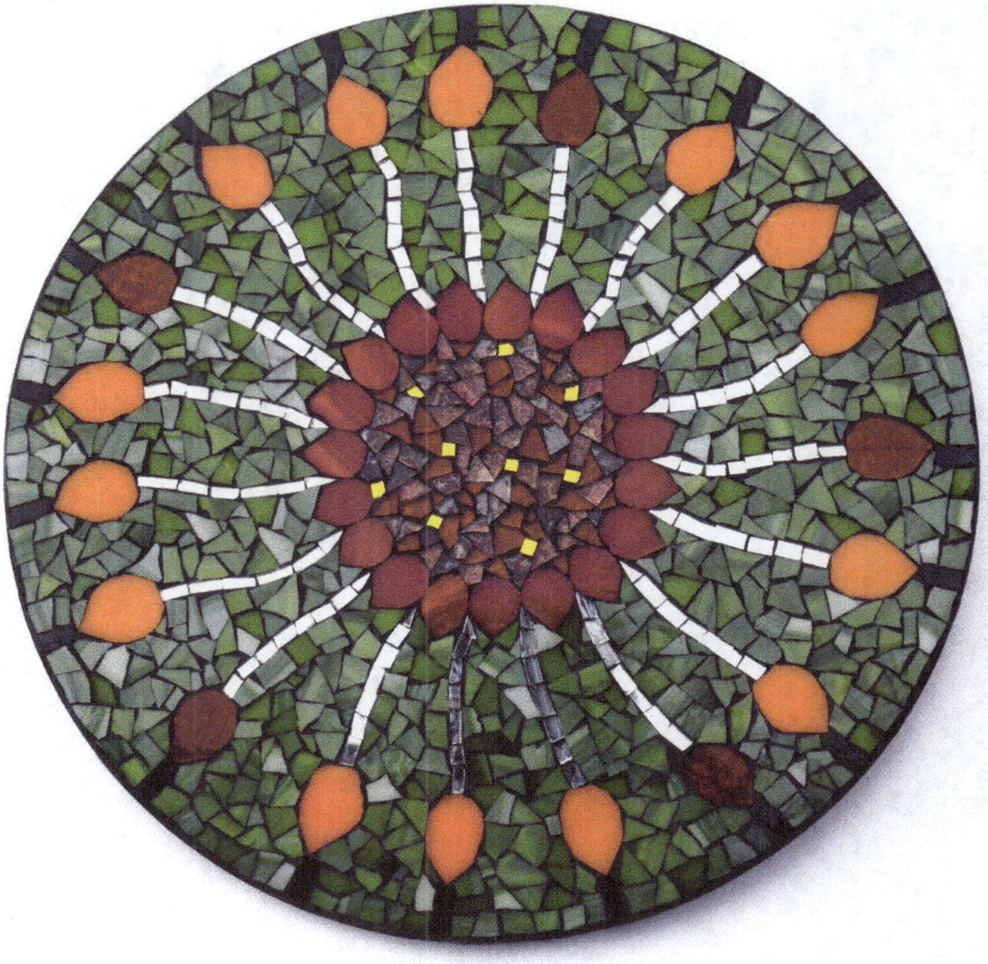

Other books from this author on Amazon:

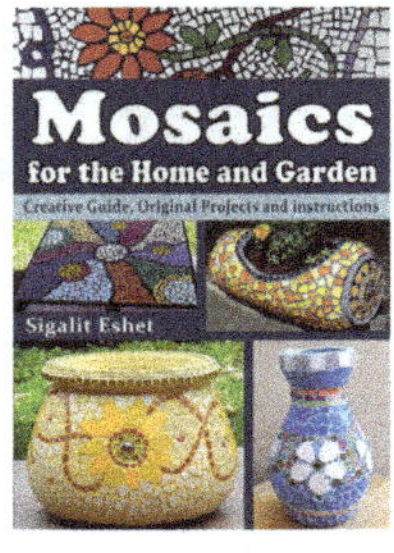 Mosaics for the Home and Garden

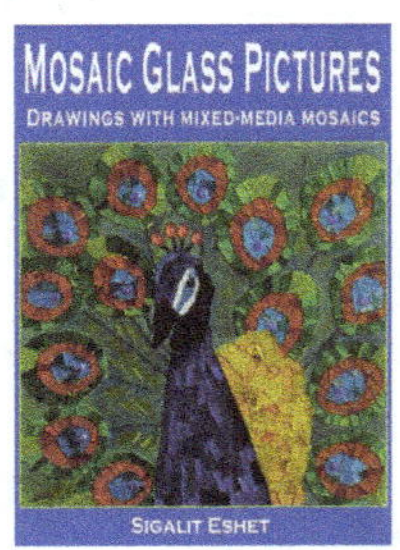 Mosaic Glass Pictures

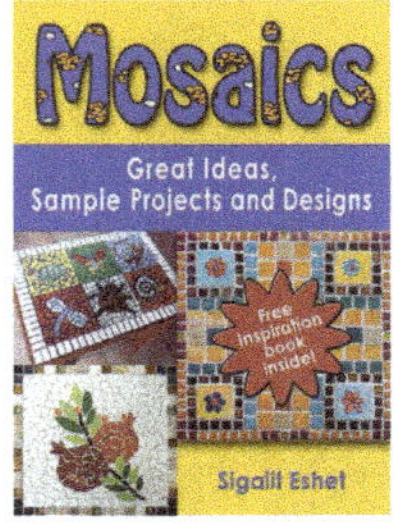 Mosaics: Great Ideas and Projects

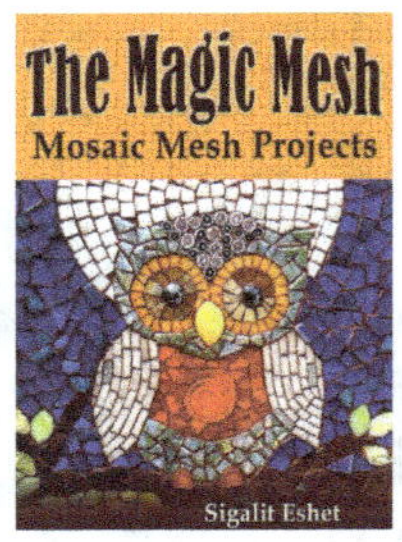 The Magic Mesh - Mosaic Mesh Projects

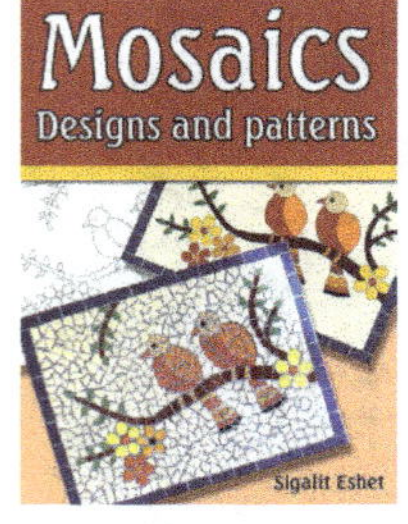 Mosaics - Designs and patterns

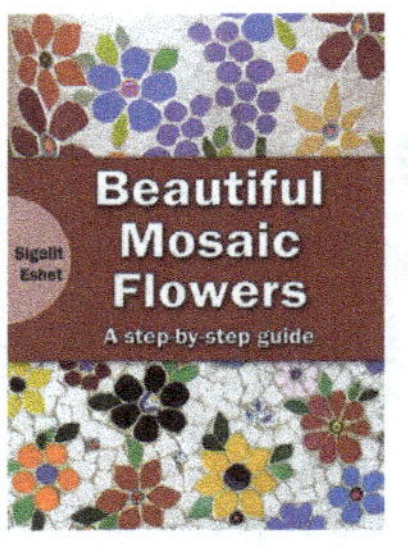 Beautiful Mosaic Flowers

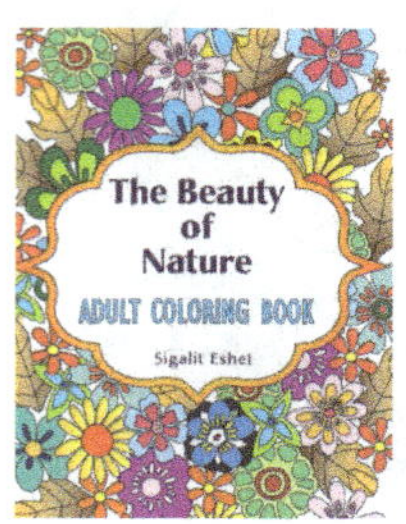 The beauty of nature: Adult coloring book